BELIEVABLE
HOPE

*FIVE ESSENTIAL ELEMENTS
TO BEAT ANY ADDICTION*

MICHAEL CARTWRIGHT

WITH KEN ABRAHAM

Health Communications, Inc.
Deerfield Beach, Florida

www.hcibooks.com

**Library of Congress Cataloging-in-Publication Data
is available through the Library of Congress.**

©2012 Michael Cartwright

ISBN 13: 978-07573-1730-9 (paperback)
ISBN 10: 0-7573-1730-8 (paperback)
ISBN 13: 978-07573-1731-6 (e-book)
ISBN 10: 0-7573-1731-6 (e-book)

Publisher: Health Communications, Inc.
    3201 S.W. 15th Street
    Deerfield Beach, FL 33442–8190

Cover design by Lee Steffen
Interior design and formatting by Lawna Patterson Oldfield

It is an honor and a privilege to dedicate this book to the two strongest influences in my life: My grandmother, Mary Sue Cartwright, who set me on the right path, and to my incredible wife, Tina Cartwright, who walks with me each day on the path, bringing help and healing to others.

To Mom and Dad, thank you, Mom, for teaching me love and compassion for our fellow human beings; and Dad, thank you for instilling in me the drive to succeed.

To the greatest joys of my life, Alexander and Ally, may the principles that have shaped my life and the stories within these pages be a positive path for you to travel as you grow into adulthood.

Love,
Dad

CONTENTS

ACKNOWLEDGMENTS

Just as a strong support group can help a person to break free from addictive behaviors, it takes a great group of coworkers to produce a book such as this. My support group in this effort has been nothing less than fantastic.

I am deeply grateful to Peter Vegso and Allison Janse of HCI Books for understanding the vision and the opportunity for Believable Hope. Thank you, Peter and Allison, for joining me in this exciting journey.

Special thanks to Rebekah Hubbell, who believed in this project from the beginning and took the initiative to get the ball rolling. I gave Rebekah a difficult opening task: I asked her to find me the best cowriter in the business. She came through with flying colors, introducing me to *New York Times* bestselling author Ken Abraham, who shaped my stories and brought them to life. Thank you, Ken, for capturing the passion I have for sharing Believable Hope!

Thanks, too, to my incredible business partners. You are the best!

To my fantastic team at American Addiction Centers, I could not do what I do without you. Together, we are making a positive difference in people's lives.

I am deeply indebted to these individuals who have participated in sharing the transformation stories in this book:

Pat McDonnell • Bob Nash • Darren Kavinoky
Jerrod Menz • Dennis Miller • Dan Cronin • Jed Wallace
Louis Gossett Jr. • Jordin Tootoo • Tony Newman • Dallas Taylor
Bree Boyce • Jessie Fortner • Khalil Rafati • Jose Orozco

Without your significant contributions, this book would not exist. Thank you for your dedication to seeing lives transformed by Believable Hope.

INTRODUCTION

*T*he young man writhed in pain on the floor of the sparse, white hospital room. The walls were melting, caving in on him, moving again in eerie undulating motions, each wave drawing closer to him, causing him to fear that he might be sucked into the plaster at any moment. His brain felt as though it had been immersed in battery acid and now threatened to explode. His skin crawled. A thousand mosquitoes and spiders chewed on his body at the same time. He flinched and jerked uncontrollably. Loud voices from invisible people screamed at him from every angle, the irritating cacophony sounding like fingernails scraping across a chalkboard; other voices whispered heinously behind him at even a moment of quiet respite.

He covered his ears with his hands, but the voices easily penetrated his palms. Indeed, the voices were already in his ears, inside his head, in his heart and soul. They threatened to maim and kill him, and at times, he wished they would.

Drug addiction had been bad enough; alcoholism had wracked his young body as well. But this was different. This was hell. Now the demons attacked his mind with a vengeance. All mental acuity acquiesced to the schizophrenia.

1

He tried to call out for help, but his parched tongue refused to cooperate. His voice died in his throat. Any sounds that managed to escape his mouth formed no sentences but dissolved into gibberish. Despair flooded over him again as it had so many times during the past several months he'd been in this room. He glanced around in a paranoid frenzy. He knew they'd be coming for him soon. The doctors. The nurses. Psychiatrists examined him daily, peering at him intensely as though he were a wild animal in a zoo. Nurses pumped his body full of drugs that were supposed to ease his anxiety, but none ever did. Instead he simply stared straight ahead, eyes wide open in a catatonic state.

When he calmed down enough to listen, he heard the doctors' and nurses' terse, fearful whispers. "He will never be well. He is going to be like this for the rest of his life. The best thing we can do for him is to keep him on strong medications. Maybe with some luck and some occupational therapy, he may be able hold down a job someday. Assuming he doesn't kill himself or overdose first."

A hopeless case.

Written off by the medical and psychiatric community. After all, they had done their best to help him, and their best efforts simply weren't good enough.

He would never amount to anything.

But he did.

How do I know?

Because I am that young man.

My name is Michael Cartwright. Don't tell me that you can't get free of drugs or alcohol or any other addiction, or that you will never be healthy and "normal" again. I know you can get well. And I will show you how.

A Tool You Can Really Use

Someone you know desperately needs this book.

Do you know a person who is leading an emotionally damaged, pain-filled life, and pretending that he or she *chooses* to live that way? Do you know someone who is dealing with an addiction or alcoholism, struggling with a weight problem, or trying to overcome some sort of compulsive behavior?

I do. Most of us do. Maybe that person we know . . . is *you*.

As my Grandma Cartwright used to say, "Everyone has something. Everyone has some challenge to overcome. It is how we deal with that challenge that determines our future and makes all the difference in our lives."

Ironically, many people who struggle with addictions or compulsive behavior patterns are not homeless, living on the streets, or sleeping on park benches or in dark alleys. They are your family members, your neighbors, or your friends. They are *us*. Many people who need profound change in their lives are living in beautiful homes, driving late-model automobiles, wearing stylish clothing, and paying for their kids to go to the best schools. By all external appearances, they seem to be leading the good life. Yet deep inside, they are controlled by compulsions they wish they could overcome. They numb their pain with alcohol, drugs, food, nicotine, excessive shopping, pornography, gambling, hoarding, and a host of other compulsive behaviors. When one method no longer brings the desired euphoria, they desperately seek something else.

The good news is that there is hope—*believable hope*, hope that is not a mere pipe dream, but actually leads to positive change. Thousands of women and men are leading active, joyful lives, free from the constraints of their formerly life-controlling behaviors. How did it happen?

They found freedom by improving their mindsets and discovering believable hope.

Whether a person is trying to get off drugs or alcohol, lose weight, overcome a persistent temptation to gamble away his life savings, turn away from pornography, or stop hoarding so much junk she can't find the floor, the key to transformation is to develop a new outlook on life. Indeed, no long-term freedom from compulsive behavior is possible without a change in a person's thinking and attitudes.

I know this truth well. Hooked on drugs and alcohol as a teenager, I landed in a catatonic state as a patient in a psychiatric hospital for five months during my early twenties. Despite rehabilitation programs and counseling, my life continued on a downward spiral until my sweet, loving grandmother hit me between the eyes with the truth. The essential truths she impressed upon me form the foundations of this book.

I'm not naively, pompously, or piously pontificating about "other people's problems." I've experienced many of these life-controlling issues as well. I empathize with you. I know how it feels to be addicted or overweight. But I'm not chained to my past anymore, and that's what gives me the confidence to encourage you—that you, too, can be free.

How did I transform my life? I got off drugs and alcohol by establishing a new mindset, fostered by advice from my grandmother and drawn from such classic books as Norman Vincent Peale's *The Power of Positive Thinking*; *Psycho-Cybernetics*, by Dr. Maxwell Maltz; *As a Man Thinketh*, by James Allen; *Alcoholics Anonymous*, also known as "The Big Book"; and dozens of other spiritually oriented works.

I don't want to toot my own horn—well, maybe just a little—but it is important that you understand why I am so confident that my approach to overcoming your life challenges will work for you. By changing my mindset, I have not only been able to overcome my addictions, I have become emotionally healthy and happy as well. Once free of my own compulsive behavior, I opened a halfway house for drug- and alcohol-addicted mentally ill victims in one of the most drug-infested neighborhoods in Nashville. At twenty-seven years of age, I established Foundations Associates, and the first of several residential drug and alcohol treatment centers, through which I have helped thousands of other people plagued by compulsive behavior. I pioneered centers in various locations across the United States to address the needs of everyday people as well as high-end, celebrity-type, and executive clients. Today, as chairman of the board of American Addiction Centers, a leader in the addiction treatment community, I have renovated and reopened The Greenhouse, a luxurious, "classic" spa property in Dallas, as well as the Desert Hope Center in Las Vegas. Additionally, I developed Fit-RX, a residential weight-loss facility and program located in Nashville. To date, thousands of people have completed rehabilitative programs at our treatment centers. Another 20,000 people contact our companies each *month* seeking information or help in dealing with some life-controlling issue.

Now, with more than twenty years of experience in dealing with addictive behavior in both "down and outers" and "up and outers," I am considered a premier addiction specialist. With my emphasis on dual diagnosis—treating addictive behavior along with the accompanying mental/emotional issues—our success rate has been so impressive that I was invited to testify before the U.S. Senate as an expert on substance abuse and mental health matters.

Through my companies, I have been involved in fifteen major federally funded independent research studies on co-occurring disorders, spanning ten years, with more than 6,000 participants. We synthesized research studies and insights from great minds in the recovery field from all across America, distilling their most effective principles and methods into a simple pattern that anyone who is truly willing to work at changing his or her life can follow. As a result, over a period of more than twenty years, we formulated the concepts and ideas in this book—sound, practical secrets that work. These are not merely theories or psychological postulates. No, the answer to beating every addiction is here.

....

The answer to beating every addiction is here.

....

A New Battlefront

In recent years, I've trained my rehabilitative crosshairs on a more subtle yet far more pervasive compulsive behavior: chronic overeating or eating poorly, combined with a lack of exercise—leading to obesity. Millions of people are overweight, setting themselves up for heart disease, diabetes, and other debilitating diseases. Again, I know this from my own experience, and will share with you how I dropped more than seventy pounds to regain a healthy lifestyle. More importantly, I will help you implement a program that can truly transform your physical life as well as your emotional life.

I'm convinced that creating a new mindset—the same approach I have developed to overcome other addictive behaviors—can help millions of people conquer their battles with the bulge. My common-sense approach to diet and exercise, combined with the real key—the change of mindset—can lead to a permanent transformation and a new quality of life.

In this book, I share my own struggle to overcome devastating addictive behaviors, including alcoholism, drug addiction, and food addictions. I'll offer practical, doable advice (gleaned as much from my grandmother as professional treatment centers) to help you overcome any compulsive behavior. This book will be a lifesaver for people battling addictive behaviors, but equally important, it will be a fresh infusion of hope for friends, family members, and others who are trying to encourage someone close to them to find the strength to live a transformed life.

Why This Book?

Since beating my own addictions, I've felt compelled to help others win their battles with self-destructive behavior. As a young man in my early twenties, I took a job as a case worker in a local drug and alcohol rehabilitation center. I soon realized that the need far surpassed the available help, especially for those people whose addictions involved some sort of mental illness. I discovered that more than 65 percent of people involved in substance abuse had a mental disorder that was not being treated. Mental illness takes a variety of forms, everything from mood disorders; thought, anxiety, and personality disorders; and eating disorders, to illnesses such as depression and schizophrenia. That's why I opened a halfway house in one of the toughest sections of Nashville, providing a place where mentally ill addicts and alcoholics could find help without condemnation. I later developed the Greenhouse, the Ritz-Carlton of research-based clinical care, in a fantastic, luxurious, resort-like property where people with compulsive behavior can get well. My entire life has been devoted to helping others get free.

This book is an extension of that purpose, by creating a nonclinical, easy-to-understand transformation tool, and providing a positive mindset that can be useful to individuals in all walks of life.

Many books are written by members of the medical community on the subjects of addictive and compulsive behaviors. Books by celebrities who have battled drug, alcohol, and weight-loss issues are plentiful as well. But rare is the book by a person who actually struggled with drug, alcohol, and food addictions, as well as mental illness, and who has overcome those problems and gone on to establish facilities and programs to help others get free. I am that person, and you are reading that book.

What Makes This Different?

What makes my approach so different? Most therapies and treatments tend to deal with the symptoms rather than the solutions. Therapy is valuable and provides marvelous help, but many people could find a whole new world of freedom if they could simply change their mindsets. Real change is possible, but it is usually more *mental* and *emotional* than clinical.

I interact with top therapists and leaders of rehabilitation programs, yet I'm constantly surprised to discover that so few of them are approaching drug and alcohol therapy this way, much less weight loss or other compulsive or life-controlling issues. We know these ideas work for success in business, but few therapists apply them to recovery issues. I do. Why? Because rehabilitation is not merely clearing your head or numbing your brain with medications, but filling your head with correct information that will allow you to develop a new mindset.

••

**Many people could find a whole new world of freedom
if they could simply change their mindsets.**

••

This emphasis on dual diagnosis, stressing the intimate connection between addictive behaviors and mental illness, has also set our approach apart from most others. Until recent years, the psychiatric field either ignored dual diagnoses or treated personality issues as the underlying causes of substance abuse in most people. They assumed that a person is a drug addict or alcoholic because of an underlying personality disturbance. They believed that abstinence from the mood-altering drugs or alcohol would cause the symptoms to disappear.

Research, however, has proven such assumptions false. Simply put, dual diagnosis goes much deeper, attempting to deal with the mental/emotional issues that not only may contribute to addictive behavior but often remain even after a person stops the behavior, if the deeper issues remain untreated. Often someone who is emotionally or mentally ill attempts to deal with life by turning to drugs, alcohol, or some other substance. Conversely, a homeless person addicted to drugs or alcohol is often mentally ill. Yes, he may be a drug addict; she may be an alcoholic, but they are mentally ill first. That's what leads to the compulsive behavior. Without addressing both sides of the equation—addiction and mental illness—it is only a matter of time before that person gets into trouble again.

Perhaps that explains why you keep slipping back into the same negative patterns, engaging in similar destructive actions, or putting up with abusive behavior on the part of someone else. Maybe you've never realized that real change is even possible.

It's easy to be placated rather than finding genuine transformation. It's much simpler to medicate our pain than it is to do the hard work that will control or eliminate the emotional triggers that cause it. That's why the use of antidepressants has increased more than 400 percent within the last decade. Stress, uncertainty, and fear in society at large all contribute to the problems of compulsive behavior. Lack of hope leads to lack of ambition, which inevitably leaves a person vulnerable to "escape" through food, alcohol, drugs, pornography, and other obsessive-compulsive behaviors.

Despite massive efforts by the government and the private sector, drug and alcohol addictions continue unabated, with another generation of young adults already addicted to nicotine, alcohol, cocaine, and a wide variety of relatively new designer drugs. Eradication is next to impossible. As long as there is a market for personality-altering substances, someone will supply them. The great need today is to educate people regarding the dangers of these substances, and to help those addicted to overcome their compulsive behavior and live transformed lives.

You Can Change for the Better

By making small, consistent, daily choices, you can change for the better—and I'm going to show you how to do it. Many people want to change, but don't know how or where to start. In the pages ahead you will find the best thinking from expert therapists actively involved in our rehabilitative treatment centers, as well as my grandmother's practical wisdom. I've honed these concepts to five elements, essential for anyone desiring permanent, positive change in his or her lifestyle. These principles are so simple that almost anyone can adopt them; they can be customized and applied to any area of life in which a person desires transformation. Yet they are so profound that most people miss them.

The five important ingredients necessary to facilitate real, lasting change are as follows:

1. Find believable hope.
2. Specifically visualize or imagine the new world you desire to create.
3. Surround yourself with winners.
4. Put your plan into action.
5. Maintain the life you love.

We'll delve into these five simple but profound truths and show you how they can work to transform your life or the life of someone you love. We'll also discover what it takes to be motivated to change and how you can help someone else who may be addicted, as well as look at the benefits of residential treatment. Most of all, we will find practical, doable ways to transform your life!

Where do you start if you want to get your life back, or help someone else get his or her life back? For me, the answer to that question started to take shape when I truly heard what my grandmother had to say. Not merely heard her voice speaking to me, but *heard* the truth of her message that reached the deepest parts of me. Grandma's secrets for conquering cravings and compulsions helped save my life. I know her wisdom can help you overcome your life challenges as well.

BELIEVABLE HOPE

With Grandma's encouragement, I was able to conquer my own mental and emotional illness, as well as addictions to alcohol, drugs, and food—which is why I have the audacity to tell you that you can get free from whatever mess in which you are mired. But for any transformation to be effective, you must first have believable hope, a reason to believe that freedom is possible.

1

Thank God for Grandma

They say that father knows best, but for me, Grandma's wisdom trumped all. Grandmother Mary Sue Cartwright saw the world differently than most people. Despite growing up in the aftermath of the Great Depression, she refused to let poverty permeate her spirit. During those difficult years following the 1929 stock market crash, Grandmother Cartwright may not have possessed much materially, but she never saw herself as "poor." Instead, she chose to see the best even in a difficult situation; she worked hard for every dime she received and believed that a better life was possible. She and my grandfather, Marion Hamilton Cartwright, knew what it felt like to have little financially, so they constantly saved for a rainy day. Grandma Cartwright worked as a clerk at the railroad in Nashville. Grandfather was employed as a tool and die maker, and in their spare time they purchased old homes and renewed them as rentals or offered them for sale. Together, they slowly built a local conglomerate of rental properties, and by the time I was born, they had amassed a small fortune.

Grandmother Cartwright was one of the most consistently positive people I've ever met. Educated at the university of hard knocks, she added to her strong work ethic a tremendous faith in God, which she nurtured regularly at the local Methodist Church. She was a marvelous example of the adage: "If you do your part, God will do His." She didn't merely sit around and wait for a miracle; she had a "get busy and do something" attitude. Yet Grandma always believed that there was a much larger plan at work in our lives, and she attempted to impart that value system to me at every opportunity.

If you do your part, God will do His.

Grandma Cartwright was a generous and giving person; she volunteered her services for everything from church work to Meals on Wheels to the Red Cross. She was constantly on the move, helping someone in need. She and my grandfather got up early every morning and were busy from sunup to sundown, perpetually working on something. Their home was spotlessly clean and neat, their yard perfectly manicured, with everything in order, a place for everything and everything in its place. Everyone in our family knew that "cleanliness is next to godliness" and that "prayer changes things." Grandma taught those principles to her kids and grandchildren, and for the most part, they caught on fairly well.

My parents had married in their early twenties, and I came along soon after. In many ways, Mom and Dad were still kids themselves and weren't really ready to deal with grown-up life. Dad had served in the U.S. Air Force during the Vietnam War, and he returned home carrying a lot of emotional baggage. Perhaps in an attempt to drown his memories of sights and sounds he'd experienced in 'Nam, Dad drank a lot, but he still managed to hold down a job with the Metro Housing Authority. Mom worked as an LPN at the county hospital.

Mom and Dad were good people, and they taught me a strong work ethic and a "never give up" attitude, but when I was five years of age, Mom and Dad divorced, and I went to live with my mother in a suburb of Nashville. Mom struggled as a single parent to provide for us, and life seemed constantly filled with tension. She went back to college to get her RN degree, which helped with our financial situation but left me alone a lot, especially when shortly after my parents' divorce was final, Dad left town. He was gone for about three years. When he returned to Nashville, Dad reconnected with me, so I had a relationship with him, but it was on an irregular basis. I stayed with him occasionally during the summer or on weekends.

My Favorite Person in the World!

But Dad's mother, Grandma Cartwright, provided consistency in my life. Grandma was my rock; she was the heroine in a storybook, the main character, convinced that people really could live happily ever after, no matter what turmoil they endured. For everything positive that I am today, I give credit to my grandmother. She was the quintessential God-fearing woman, always loving and kind, with a confident approach to life. Grandma had a real gift of encouragement. She seemed to know innately that heaping more condemnation on a person rarely changes him or her for the better. Instead, Grandma dished out sincere and honest appreciation at every opportunity. In a million simple and seemingly insignificant ways, she chose to emphasize the positive things in life, rather than the negative. Despite the fact that Grandfather Cartwright died due to a heart attack in the early 1970s, Grandmother remained upbeat. She was uplifting and fun to be around. She made me feel special, and consequently—as an only child with divorced parents—I became even more attached to Grandma. She was my absolute favorite person in the world.

Grandma did her best to keep me on the straight and narrow path, providing a moral compass, and helping Mom and Dad to pay for me to attend Catholic school, since that was my mom's religious denomination. But the environment in which a person lives has a profound impact, and during my early years, I felt the tension in our home. My mom's side of the family owned a bar, a popular local Nashville hangout, so I regarded drinking as normal; I didn't realize how destructive the abuse of alcohol could be.

Slipping into Addiction

I had early and easy access to a variety of mind-altering substances. I wasn't alone; many of my young friends did, too. For me, Dad was not an integral part of my everyday life, and with Mom working so much, I was on my own for hours each day, once I left the purview of the teachers at school. I was an accident waiting to happen.

During my teenage years, the drinking and drugs got worse. The escalation had more to do with my personality than peer pressure or my parents. Even to this day, everything I do, I throw myself into it, doing it to the nth degree, often going to extremes. So once I started drinking, I kept on drinking until I was plastered; once I began dabbling in drugs, I soon graduated to using more and stronger drugs, which exacerbated my addiction, since I constantly needed more to maintain the same sense of euphoria I formerly felt with much smaller, "safer" substances. In no time at all, the drugs and alcohol took over my life, but I didn't see the warning signs. As far as I was concerned, I was simply the best partier in my school.

It was only when I went to Grandma's house that I sensed the dichotomy between what Grandma believed of me and expected for me, and the downward spiral of my day-to-day life. I relished visiting Grandmother Cartwright, and her home was always a place of peace for me. I could hardly wait to get there, and once there, I was reluctant to leave. Having my grandmother as a guiding light was invaluable. She doled out down-to-earth wisdom and expressed a rare depth of human understanding. She created a different sort of atmosphere in which I could breathe in good things and grow. She recognized that I needed to get out of my current environment at high school, so she encouraged me to entertain lofty dreams of becoming a military officer and eventually a lawyer.

With Mom and Dad's help, and some extra funds from a football scholarship, I attended a military academy for the last portion of my high school education. But I didn't change my ways. In fact, I partied so much in high school that I missed my own graduation. While all my family members were gathered at the ceremony, I was passed out in a hotel room. From that point on, I was hell-bent on self-destruction. I started drinking even more heavily and using drugs more frequently.

I enrolled in a state university because my parents and grandparents said they would help support me through school as long as I worked hard, got decent grades, and maintained a high grade point average. I worked hard all right, but not at academics. I spent my first semester of college partying as heartily as I could. At the end of the semester, I brought home straight "Incompletes," which turned to Fs when I failed to make up the work. By the next semester, I had flunked out of college.

It was time for me to get a job—well, actually, I had no choice. Neither Mom nor Dad, not even Grandma Cartwright would support a lazy loafer, so I talked my uncle into hiring me as part of his construction crew. I worked construction jobs for about four months before concluding, *This is not the life for me!* I decided to go back to college, this time paying for it myself.

I reenrolled in college but fared little better. Although I was popular among my peers and the life of every party, I couldn't wrap my alcohol-logged brain around the academics. Before long, I dropped out of school again. I decided to try a private university, and for a while I made good grades, but all too soon, I slipped back into my same self-destructive patterns and quit school again.

I couldn't believe my life had turned out so poorly; I felt that I was created to do more and be more, and I wanted more out of life. My grandmother had instilled in me a belief that I could do anything I wanted to do and be anything I wanted to be. She taught me from my early years that I was special, that I had a destiny to fulfill, that I was supposed to do something important in life. She believed that, and she believed in me. I knew that I was not living up to her hopes and dreams for me. *This isn't what Grandma meant for me to be,* I thought.

Grandma, however, kept pouring into me believable hope. "You're going to be something important, Michael," she emphasized. I didn't know what she hoped I might be, but knowing that Grandma wanted more for me and expected better of me helped tip the balance when I considered making a change.

2

Hitting Bottom

Every week, I meet someone who says, "Michael, you don't understand. You're a successful businessman with a great family and a wonderful life. You can't possibly understand what I'm going through. I'm depressed. I drink too much. I can't shake the drugs. I'm trapped in a negative life. You don't realize how tough it is for me to overcome my compulsive behavior."

Oh? Really? As an eighteen-year-old, I had gotten so delusional that one day I pulled my car into Nashville's West End Catholic Church parking lot, and with the car in "park," I simply sat there with my foot on the accelerator, afraid to let up on the pedal because I was convinced that if I did, a bomb would explode in the car. For a long time, I sat there with the engine revved, the throttle fully open, the car roaring loudly in the parking lot.

Finally, I mustered the courage to open the door and dive out of the vehicle. The engine immediately calmed to a quiet purr, and much to my surprise, the car did not blow up. I picked myself up off the pavement and stumbled toward the closest doors of the church. Once inside I found a priest and told him my story. He arranged for me to be seen by a doctor in Parthenon Pavilion Hospital, where the doctors diagnosed me with paranoid schizophrenia. I spent two weeks in the hospital. I left with a batch of prescriptions, but nothing else in my life had substantially changed.

Two years later, I broke again, this time in Florida. For a while, I had stayed off drugs and alcohol and had joined the military. When I entered the service, I checked off "No" on the form asking if I had any history of mental illness. I'm sorry now, but lying came all too naturally to me in those days. I had attended a military high school and was in good physical condition, so I doubt that anyone even checked into the details of my previous hospitalization. Later, I would be diagnosed with cyclic psychosis, a rare malady that mimics schizophrenia. My father suffered from a similar disease, as did my grandfather. Both men served their country well and had outstanding military careers, although they too found themselves in hospitals on more than one occasion, needing anti-psychotic medications simply to bring them back to their base lines. Perhaps because of their experience, I felt no qualms in signing up for the military.

I did well for about three months, and was preparing to attend Navy SEALs school, but then I became delusional and paranoid and had a psychotic break again. I felt as though I was in a scary movie, or a Vincent van Gogh painting; the walls were melting, people were talking about killing me. Everywhere I looked, people were out there trying to get me. I was catatonic; I couldn't speak.

I was admitted to a psychiatric hospital in Orlando, and remained there for several months. I was in despair. Totally frayed and frazzled, I had suffered a psychotic break in which I felt as though somebody had poured battery acid over my brain. Exacerbating matters further, I was terrified because I couldn't control my body's responses.

The psychiatrists ordered a variety of heavy-duty medications designed to reduce my anxiety, but I was so delusional I refused to take the medicine, because I was convinced that the drugs were poison. When my mom and a girlfriend finally convinced me to try the medication, rather than causing me to feel better, I felt worse. Now, I realized that I had been living in delusion for months. *This is hell*, I thought. I had no desire to get out of bed; I couldn't handle a menial job such as washing dishes at a restaurant or mowing lawns. I couldn't sit in a classroom or think clearly enough to take a class in school. The teacher's voice got garbled among the various other voices I was hearing, taunting me, talking to me and about me. I couldn't think, my words came out as gibberish. I didn't want to live like this.

I wanted to die.

When the doctors discharged me after five months, I walked out of the hospital with a stack of prescriptions, still feeling depressed and despondent, and still on heavy doses of antipsychotic medications.

Go Pull Some Weeds

I went back home to Nashville. As always, one of the first people I wanted to see was Grandmother Cartwright. We sat down together in her living room, and I tried to explain to her what had happened to me over the past five or six months and how miserable I still felt. Grandmother listened to my sad story empathetically, and she commiserated with me, but she wasn't about to let me wallow in my own poop.

"Michael," Grandma paused to make sure she had my full attention, then continued. "Everybody has *something*, some struggle, some trauma, some issue with which they have to deal." She looked deeply into my eyes. "It's how you deal with that something that makes you who you are."

"But, Grandmother, what am I going to do? I'd have a hard time getting a job or making it through college. I don't have anything going for myself."

"Well, honey, at least you have your legs. You have your sight. Let's get out a sheet of paper and list all the positives, all the good things you still have in life."

"Grandmother!" I said, the exasperation in my voice all too evident. "I'm hearing things. The medication I'm taking makes me feel so zonked out, I can hardly keep my eyes open. I'm depressed over everything that has happened. My whole world has crashed down around me. I thought I was going to become a Navy SEAL and now that dream has gone away, too, and you want me to list all the *positives* in my life? What positives? I'm sorry. I can't seem to find any."

"Oh, of course you can, Michael. Let's write them all down." She reached into a desk and pulled out a yellow tablet pad. "Let's think about it. You still can see. Here, write this down, 'I still have my sight.'" She handed the tablet and a pen to me.

I knew it was useless to argue with Grandmother, and I respected her too much to complain, so I dutifully took the pen and wrote, "I can see," on the tablet.

"Good!" Grandmother gushed as though we'd just won the Publishers Clearinghouse Sweepstakes. "Now, what else are you grateful for?"

"I can walk. I still have my legs," I said.

"That's right. Yes, indeed. That's at least two things that you can be thankful for. Write that down."

I scribbled the words on the pad.

"What else?" Grandmother prompted.

"I still have you to help me."

"Oh, yes. That's a very good one. Put that down on paper."

We continued like that for a half hour or more. Every time I got stymied, Grandmother interjected something else for which I could give thanks. After a while she said, "You just need to go pull some weeds. Come on outside and help me. Get your eyes off yourself for a while, do some hard work, and you'll feel much better." I reluctantly went outside and helped Grandma pull the weeds out of her flower garden. I totally missed the point that in reality I was pulling weeds out of my own life. But that day was the beginning of a major turn-around in my life.

Everybody has something, some struggle, some trauma, some issue with which they have to deal.

Grandmother gave me a book to read, *The Power of Positive Thinking*, and I was captivated by the stories. The pages were filled with simple stories of ordinary people who had found real purpose in their lives, healing for their pains, freedom from their self-imposed constraints, and a new outlook on the future. Inside, my heart pounded with excitement as I said to myself, *Yes! That is what I want.*

> Believe you can, and you can. Belief is one of the most powerful of problem dissolvers. When you believe that a difficulty can be overcome, you are more than halfway to victory over it already.
>
> —*Norman Vincent Peale*

I wish I could say that I took Grandma's advice to heart and my life was instantly transformed. But true transformation usually doesn't work that way, and unfortunately, before long, I slipped right back into the same patterns. By the time I began contemplating changing my lifestyle, I had been in several psychiatric hospitals. I had mental illness as well as alcohol and drug problems. Everything about my life looked as though I would end up in jail, a drug addict or an alcoholic, or a hopeless, homeless bum living on the streets. I was going for broke—and I almost made it.

A Fresh Start

It doesn't take a lot to develop believable hope—the absolutely essential, critically necessary belief that you can actually make a fresh start—but it must come from somewhere, and it usually requires a source outside yourself. I had one person who was dropping positive autosuggestions into my mind: *You are a good person. You can have a good life.* That person was Grandmother Cartwright.

I never forgot the things that she poured into me, but I regret that I fooled around and wasted so much time before taking her words to heart. When the light finally came on for me, I was nearly twenty-four years old. I was lying in bed after an all-night bender when a voice in my mind said, "You are better than this. Your life is worth more than drowning in alcohol and drugs."

My mind was racing, my heart pounding. I sensed that I was at a crossroads. "Please, God. I'll do anything," I prayed.

A thought formulated in my mind, and something seemed to say to me, "Go to an Alcoholics Anonymous meeting." I took that as an answer to my prayer.

I searched out the location of an Alcoholics Anonymous group, and the very next day I went to my first AA meeting. For more than ninety days, I attended at least one meeting and sometimes two every single day. That might not have happened had my grandmother not instilled within me a believable hope that I could change. From that first AA meeting to today, I've not had another drink or used any form of illegal drugs.

Believable Hope, the Critical Element

You must have believable hope that transformation is possible. But what is *believable hope*, and how can you find it?

Believable hope, in contrast to mere positive affirmations espoused by motivational speakers, preachers, and politicians, is based on evidence that change has been experienced by others in conditions similar to yours and is absolutely possible for you. It helps to have some positive role models, mentors, or sponsors, or some reason to believe that you can actually change.

....

Believable hope is hope based on evidence that change has been experienced by others in conditions similar to yours and is absolutely possible for you.

....

Where can you find believable hope in your life, or in the lives of people you are trying to help? How can you develop believable hope (or help someone else to develop it) if you don't already have it?

Reading books about it, attending seminars, viewing and listening to audio/video materials, talking with others who have overcome life challenges—all of these are helpful. One of the most effective means of developing believable hope is to enroll in a residential program where you can immerse yourself in a new mindset. Sometimes simply knowing that somebody believes in you provides the believable hope that you can be better.

> The first step to becoming is to will it.
>
> —*Mother Teresa*

Many people discover believable hope when they seek help from a Higher Power, a power greater than themselves. That's what happened to Tony Newman.

When Tony first showed up at our treatment center, wanting to help serve addicts and alcoholics by driving our van transporting patients, I had no idea that he was one of the world's premier musicians. He was also a former drug addict and alcoholic who nearly destroyed himself.

Tony grew up in London with alcoholic parents, so it wasn't surprising that he began drinking by the time he was thirteen years of age. He began playing drums about the same time. Playing in the band represented freedom to the teenager, and alcohol represented acceptance with his bandmates. He turned professional around age seventeen, and by that time he was full-fledged alcoholic. Every time he drank, he got drunk, but because he was so talented, despite his drinking, he was able to get good jobs.

Hanging out with musicians, one of the band members said, "Let's go down to the pub."

That seemed like a good idea to Tony. "What do you drink?" the young musician asked when they arrived.

"We drink Dairy Maid." The beer bottle label displayed a young woman milking a cow. The implied message was that drinking beer was as safe as drinking milk. Safe or not, Tony got smashed.

To his alcohol consumption, Tony added a form of speed that "felt almost like two thousand beers." He quickly found that he could not take speed and play drums well. Nor could he play drunk. As the quintessential professional with a goal of being the world's best and fastest drummer, it embarrassed Tony so much that he played poorly when he drank, he adjusted his drinking patterns. He did the first show, then had two or three beers, but would not get drunk. Then following the second show, he would get plastered.

In the early 1960s, Tony was playing with the iconic Little Richard when he met a rising band from Liverpool known as the Beatles. By 1963, Tony was flying high, literally. He was playing with some of the premier music groups in the world, but spent most of his earnings on alcohol.

In the mid-'60s, Tony played with a band known as Sounds Incorporated, touring with the Beatles. Most musicians at least tried to straighten up when they came home off the road, but not Tony. For him, life was truly consumed by sex, drugs, and rock and roll. He was never fully present with his wife and young son.

Never did anyone attempt to help Tony deal with his drinking and drugging. In 1969, Jeff Beck called Tony to play for him. Tony performed at Woodstock and hung out with some of the most famous rock musicians of his day, many of whom were stoned; heroin and cocaine were the drugs of choice that weekend.

The drinking continued, as Tony wrecked one sports car after another. In three successive weekends, he crashed three priceless vehicles. He rationalized that it was simply a streak of bad luck. Tony recalls, "I didn't get in trouble every time I drank, but every time I got in trouble, I was drunk or high."

In 1976, Tony played a live concert with David Bowie in Philadelphia. The record company was recording the concert, but that didn't prevent Tony from stuffing his nose with cocaine prior to going on stage. Tony recalls, "I couldn't possibly pack any more cocaine into my nose. It was blocked solid. I didn't know where I was, and could hardly find the stage. *Where am I?* My mind was flying in several directions at once. I felt like I was in a round-about with five different exits and I couldn't tell which one to take."

Years later, Bowie rereleased the album digitally. They remixed the recording and David cleaned up some of the vocals and guitars, but he left Tony's drums totally intact.

David asked Tony to come back and work with him and write some songs. Tony was so out of it, he gave Bowie a list of demands including a steep daily rate as well as transportation by means of a private jet and all sorts of foolish perks. Essentially, Tony turned Bowie down because it would interfere with his drinking and drugging.

The downward spiral in Tony's life continued in 1978 when he moved to Nashville. By that time he had left his wife and kids, and had actually attempted getting clean, to no avail. He played with various groups and in studio recordings on numerous hit records, but he was lethargic and didn't want to work. All he wanted to do was drink and do drugs; worse yet, he was beginning to become shaky and had the DTs. He was at war with everyone, and most of all, he was at war with himself.

He had been playing with rock groups and punk rock groups in England, but in Music City, he took a job with country artist Crystal Gayle. The style of music had no calming influence on Tony. He was out of control, drinking, drugging, getting naked on airplanes, and acting out in every outlandish way anyone suggested. Tony was obsessed with always getting more—more of sex, drugs, and alcohol—but found he was receiving less and less satisfaction from his overindulgence. He tried drinking just enough to keep himself leveled out, but it never worked that way. A girlfriend took Tony to a twelve-step meeting. Tony and the woman left the meeting and went out and got drunk.

One night at a bar, the bartender told a friend of Tony's, "That Tony Newman. He's not going to be with us much longer."

Not long after that, Tony whipped his young son with a stick. When he realized what he had done, the horror of his actions brought Tony to his knees. Tony Newman was ready to change. *This has got to stop*, Tony told himself.

But not before he had one more binge.

Tony and a friend holed up in a Nashville hotel, drinking and using drugs for days, so much so that they were spitting up blood. "I can't do this anymore," Tony said. Tony's friend drove him to a local rehabilitation center, where Tony checked in and began the detoxification process. He joined the twelve-step program at the center.

One day, Tony's counselors told him to go outside and pray to a loving, Higher Power and ask for help. Tony did. He went outside, looked up, and admitted, "I'm powerless over alcohol. My life is totally unmanageable. Please help me." The keys to sobriety were his willingness to ask for help and his willingness to change.

"Give me all your burdens," Tony sensed the Higher Power speaking to him. So Tony did. He prayed in almost childlike faith, "Help." That simple prayer provided Tony the believable hope he needed to stop drinking and doing drugs. Within two weeks, Tony was free of the drugs and alcohol that had ruled his life for decades. All of his crutches were gone.

Now he had to learn how to live clean. He discovered that getting sober involved more than merely laying down the drugs and alcohol. He had to get sober sexually; he had to get sober financially; he had to get sober emotionally with his family members, especially his wife.

The next thirty days were difficult, but Tony refused to drink or do drugs. His maintenance plan was simple. He asked for help. He has done the same thing every morning since—he has simply asked for help. Today, Tony has been clean and sober for more than twenty-eight years. He changed people, places, and things, especially his obsession with drugs, alcohol, and sex. "As the counselors told me," Tony quips, 'There's a slip under every skirt.'"

Once he left the treatment facility, Tony found it was important to be willing to separate himself from people, places, or things that might pull him back toward a life of drugs and alcohol. Because of his diligence, Tony has never had a relapse. He is committed to not drinking or using drugs. "I choose to ask for help every morning," Tony says. "I use deep breathing exercises and prayer when I feel myself getting anxious. I take five or ten deep breaths, breathing and praying, and it helps me to refocus my mind on what I want, rather than what I don't want."

Tony readily acknowledges that by calling out to a loving Higher Power, he found the believable hope he needed to make lasting, positive changes in his life. Today, Tony is married to a master's-level clinician who runs a major rehabilitation center. Tony works as a house manager at a treatment facility in Las Vegas. He still plays drums, and his children are carrying on his legacy as a world-class drummer.

"I've made amends as best I can," Tony admits, "so I don't live in the past. I can't change the insane things I have done. I can only make good choices in the future."

> God enters by a private door into each individual.
>
> —*Ralph Waldo Emerson*

Tim Sanders, the former chief solutions officer at Yahoo!, and currently the CEO of Net Minds, is the author of the book *Love Is the Killer App*. Tim says, "My faith in God has given me incredible resiliency. When you have faith in a Higher Power, you cannot, *will* not fail."[1] I agree.

Discovering believable hope motivates a person to reach out and help someone else. In fact, since substance abusers, alcoholics, and people who are prone to life-controlling issues are notoriously self-absorbed, it is a good sign that you are on the right path when you sense the desire within you to help someone facing a battle you have already encountered.

I was pleasantly surprised one day when I saw Oscar– and Emmy Award–winning movie star Sir Anthony Hopkins show up as a volunteer at one of our treatment centers, willing to mentor other men who were in a recovery program struggling with alcoholism. Tony Hopkins understood their dilemma well.

He described his own battle with the bottle in terms closely akin to some of the exorcisms the celebrated actor has conducted on the big screen—the difference being, Anthony's demons were real. In recounting his drinking problem, he confessed, "It was like being possessed by a demon, an addiction, and I could not stop."

In his desperation, Anthony asked for help, and a woman told him to trust in God. Although he considered himself an atheist at that time, Anthony Hopkins humbled himself. "I said, 'Well, why not?'" the actor told CNN's Piers Morgan in an interview.

"I was hell-bent on destruction. And I just asked for a little bit of help, and suddenly, pow! It was just like, bingo," the actor recalled. To date, Sir Anthony has been sober for more than thirty-five years, thanks to discovering help from Above. Besides expertly portraying fascinating characters in movies, Anthony Hopkins often volunteers to help others fighting the demons of alcoholism and addictions.

"It was such a quantum leap, from this to that," Hopkins acknowledged.[2] That is believable hope.

The Powerful Influence of a Mentor

Believable hope is the essential foundation upon which positive change can be built, and one of the best ways to groom believable hope is by finding and emulating a mentor. A mentor's experience often can provide a positive frame of reference. A good mentor will cause you to say, "If that person can change, so can I." Being surrounded by people who have made the same sort of positive changes that you desire, and who will encourage you to do something similar, is invaluable in producing believable hope. You have to truly believe that you not only *can* change, but you *will*.

Testimonies in church can inspire you to have faith. The value of sponsors in Alcoholics Anonymous is similar; the support systems of the most successful weight-loss programs all incorporate the power of personal examples. On the other hand, those who have never seen people who have achieved their goals have more difficulty believing it is possible.

> Optimism is the faith that leads to achievement. Nothing can be done without hope and confidence.
>
> —Helen Keller

It Can't Be Done . . .
Until You Believe It Can Be Done

For years, nobody in the world of track and field thought it humanly possible to run a mile in less than four minutes. Nobody, that is, until Roger Bannister, a twenty-five-year-old British medical student, did it. Once Bannister broke the four-minute barrier, the number of runners who have accomplished that goal has soared. What changed?

Nothing, except the runners now had believable hope that a four-minute mile was possible.

You need some frame of reference to foster belief. Think about it: Prior to July 1969, many people did not believe it was possible to travel to the moon. But once Neil Armstrong and Buzz Aldrin landed on the Sea of Tranquility, stepped out and kicked up some moon dust, and planted an American flag on the surface, every little boy and girl in the United States knew that it was possible to travel to the moon and beyond.

Why is *The Biggest Loser* television program so inspiring? Because we can see heavily overweight people on television losing weight in a progressive manner, going from 500 pounds to 200 pounds. Something within us says, "If he did it, I can do it, too." Suddenly, you have a frame of reference that gives you hope. You have to believe that you can get up out of the gutter, that you can go from sick and homeless to healthy and prosperous.

If you don't have believable hope, you won't have a tangible target at which to aim. You won't know where you are going, or what the goal is, and even if you do, you won't believe the goal is achievable. For a goal to become a reality, you must believe that you can accomplish it. Or you never will.

In the process of developing believable hope, beware of setting unrealistic goals. Some people want to lose fifty pounds in a week, and that simply isn't going to happen. The change has to be incremental, with a workable plan and progressive results, to become permanent.

If my grandmother hadn't have been a stabilizing force in my life, I may not have believed a stable life was possible. Had I not known some friends whose parents were wealthy, I may not have imagined that it was possible for a guy like me to have anything other than a meager existence. But armed with the knowledge that a meaningful life was possible, I wanted it.

Alcoholics Anonymous encourages getting a sponsor because it helps to be around someone who has done what you hope to do. The same is true with weight loss. If you hope to lose weight, get around people who have lost weight and figure out what they did to accomplish their goals. Allow their experience to build believable hope within you. When I wanted to lose a significant amount of weight, my friends Darren and Dan gave me the believable hope I needed. Darren had once been an overweight kid, just like me, but he had lost the weight, and that inspired me to believe that I could slim down as well. My friend Dan confronted me about being overweight, and was a constant encouragement to me. Because of them, I recognized my problem and took steps to overcome it.

3

The Person in
the Mirror

Have you ever wondered why Alcoholics Anonymous has been so successful in helping people from all walks of life get free of alcohol? Founded in 1935 by two men identified only as Bill W., a New York stockbroker, and Dr. Bob S., a surgeon—both of whom had long histories of irresponsible drinking—the men discovered that it was possible to maintain their sobriety if they steadfastly held to twelve basic principles. From the beginning Alcoholics Anonymous emphasized Step One and Step Two as nonnegotiable steps to freedom:

> **Step One:** We admitted we were powerless over alcohol—that our lives had become unmanageable.
> **Step Two:** Came to believe that a Power greater than ourselves could restore us to sanity.
> —*Alcoholics Anonymous World Services, Inc.*

These two steps have been essential to AA's phenomenal success, and they are the basis for my own system of believable hope, and the reason for my confidence that the answer to beating any sort of addiction or compulsive behavior begins here.

Admit That You Have a Problem

Simply put: If you want to transform your life, the place to start is by admitting that *you* have an issue. The problem is yours, not someone else's; you must take responsibility. Many of the clients whom I encounter have been decimated by drug addiction or alcoholism. They have lost their jobs and their families, and some have been living in despair on the street. *What's it going to take,* we wonder, *before they are willing to change?* Surely the lightbulb is going to shine in their minds, causing them to decide to do something differently. But it doesn't.

Similarly, with weight issues, you would think that when a man cannot fit into extra-extra-large-sized shirts or a size 50 pair of pants, something would stir inside, saying, "I need to lose some weight." But often it doesn't.

Stephanie, a woman in her mid-forties, thought she could beat her obesity problem by having her jaw wired shut for several months. The operation was a success, and Stephanie survived on liquids and soft foods, and she did lose weight. But within a few months after the wires were removed, Stephanie's weight bloated upward again. She had temporarily changed her eating habits, but she had done nothing to change her mindset, so she remained obese.

Many people are accustomed to talking or buying their way out of a crisis. Sometimes their wealth or celebrity can be their own worst enemy. At our drug and alcohol rehabilitation centers, we treat a lot of famous personalities and celebrities. Some of the toughest people to deal with are the super rich. I recall one billionaire who got out of his limousine and sauntered into the facility as though he were Donald Trump looking for a new acquisition. Our staff made him comfortable and immediately went to work helping him to get clean. When I saw him a few days later, I greeted him in a friendly and professional manner.

"Are you the owner here?" he huffed.

"Yes, I am."

"Hmmph, I like this place," he said. "I want to buy it."

Accustomed to the bombast and bluster that oftentimes accompany addictive personalities, I smiled and downplayed his remark. "Thanks, but it is not for sale."

"But I want to buy it!" he said, sounding almost like a spoiled brat.

"Let me rephrase it," I said. "It's not for sale to you. You have only been here a few days."

He looked at me incredulously, as if to say, "My money is good everywhere else. What's wrong with you?" He was accustomed to getting anything and everything he wanted, simply because he was wealthy—but money can't buy many of the things that really matter in life.

When we were finally able to help him get honest about his life, and to admit that *he* had a problem, he was able to turn the corner and make positive changes to overcome his compulsive behaviors.

You Don't Have to Hit Bottom Before Seeking Help

Not everyone has to hit rock bottom before he or she seeks help. Indeed, thanks to modern approaches to treatment, as well as high-quality treatment centers, we've been able to raise the bottom for a lot of people hoping to overcome alcohol or drugs or other life-controlling issues.

Renowned interventionist Dan Cronin says, "Many twelve-step programs purport that a person has to hit bottom before he or she will ever change. I don't believe that. We've been able to raise the bottom so people do not have to lose everything before being motivated to change.

"A lot of people with whom I deal will never hit bottom. Their families can't cut them off from the money, because these clients *are* the money. He or she is the source of the affluence. We can't scare them into sobriety. You have to talk to them about quality of life issues, rather than hitting bottom."[3]

That was precisely true in Jordin Tootoo's life. He grew up playing ice hockey in the frigid Canadian Arctic Circle and became the first athlete of Inuit descent to make it to the National Hockey League, immediately establishing himself as a fan favorite of the NHL's Nashville Predators in 2001. With his quick smile and feisty play, he was a popular role model for youth in his native land, as well as his adopted hometown of Nashville.

But the social side of professional sports and the gritty underbelly of his chosen sport of hockey eventually took a toll on the star. Having grown up in a home where both his parents and most of his friends used alcohol, Jordin thought nothing of having a few drinks. As Jordin told me, "Booze and hockey go together. There's always going to be beer involved; hockey players and beer go hand in hand." By 2010, Jordin was drinking far too much, far too often, getting loaded on days when he was not on the ice, and going to work hung over. "It wasn't like I'd wake up craving a drink, but when we had days off, it was a green light for me to drink. Before long, I was binge drinking."

Nobody confronted Jordin about his drinking, but some of his teammates encouraged him to figure out what was going on in his life.

By Christmas 2010, Jordin had had enough. "The first step was admitting that I had a problem," he recalled. He felt that he was not only disappointing himself, he was letting down his family. He wasn't worried about losing his lifestyle or becoming a skid-row bum, but it was a matter of personal pride for him. Finally, he made up his mind. He was ready to change. He voluntarily entered inpatient care as part of the NHL's Substance Abuse and Behavioral Health Program.

Jordin didn't know what to expect when he initially went for treatment. He spent four weeks working with Dr. Brian Shaw and Dr. Dave Lewis, as well as interventionist Dan Cronin. During that time Jordin dumped his demons on the table, reflecting on the decisions he'd made and where his young life had taken him. Cronin was a no-nonsense interventionist who held up a mirror to Jordin so he could more accurately see himself.

"It was tough to hear," Jordin recalled, "but Dan was willing to tell me straight up."

During his party days, Jordin had more friends than he could count, but as soon as the booze was gone, so were many of Jordin's friends. When Jordin returned home from rehab, clean and sober, he found out who his true friends were—those who wanted to be with him for who he was, not the buzz or high his money could provide.

Jordin still enjoys attending social events, but he has learned to substitute good activities, rather than allowing himself to gravitate toward places, people, and things that he knows can rob him not only of his game but of the life he wants to live. "I'm a better person now," Jordin admitted. "I am a better professional, and I now get things done, rather than procrastinating. I don't even have a desire to drink anymore."

Jordin's parents still drink, as do most of his old friends, but for Jordin, his drinking days are over and done. "I tell my parents, 'Don't change because of me.' I don't try to preach to them, or to anyone else, but I know they are happy for me."

Jordin now finds positive ways to keep busy, and even mundane daily chores and responsibilities are a pleasure. Hunting and fishing provide him opportunities for positive recreation as well as time for making sure his mind is clear and stable. "That's where everything stems from," Jordin noted. "That mental transformation makes all the difference." Jordin Tootoo found the secret of believable hope.

> It is the mind that maketh good or ill; that maketh wretch or happy, rich or poor.
>
> —*Edmund Spenser*

We All Deal with Something

The moment I sat down for lunch with Louis Gossett Jr. at one of our treatment centers in Malibu, I recognized a man who had endured great pain. Perhaps best known for his portrayal of Sergeant Emil Foley in the blockbuster movie *An Officer and a Gentleman*, starring opposite Richard Gere and Debra Winger, Lou had allowed Hollywood's racism to push him deeper into personal isolation, and had attempted to ignore the prejudice-laced insults by numbing the pain through alcohol, drugs, and promiscuous women. Indeed, because of his penchant for easy women, Louis became an easy prey for drug dealers who proffered the women as an appetizer for "more sophisticated" drugs.

Born in the Coney Island section of Brooklyn, Gossett attended Abraham Lincoln High School, where he was a top student and class president, as well as a stellar athlete who earned letters in three sports, including basketball, for which he won all-city honors. Throughout Louis's early years, his heroes were his father and his uncles, whose lifestyles revolved around drinking and partying. They would go to work all week, then carouse on the weekends, letting out their frustrations—and they had a lot of frustrations to vent. They instilled in Louis the mindset that "you are not a man unless you can party on Friday and Saturday nights, but still get up and go to church on Sunday and work on Monday."

A high school drama teacher suggested that Louis audition for a role in the school play. Louis not only won the role, he performed so powerfully, his teacher suggested he try his luck in an open casting call on Broadway for the production of *Take a Giant Step*. Sixteen-year-old Louis Gossett Jr. won the role over four hundred other actors. The show ran for seven and a half months, and Louis received the Best Newcomer Award, topping actors Ben Gazzara and James Dean.

Still a teenager, Louis attended New York University on a basketball and drama scholarship. A big young man, at six foot four, 200 pounds, he starred not only in dozens of theatrical productions but also on the basketball court, and was invited to try out for the New York Knicks. About that same time, he won a coveted Broadway role opposite Sidney Poitier in *A Raisin in the Sun*, so he left his dreams of basketball stardom on the hardwood and moved to Greenwich Village.

The Village was homogeneous, a multiracial, Bohemian environment where Louis experienced surprisingly few prejudices. Because of his love for music, Louis gravitated toward the folk and jazz musicians such as Joan Baez, Carole King, and Richie Havens, as well as fledgling actors such as Richard Pryor, Marilyn Monroe, and Harvey Keitel. For a while, Louis emceed a music show at a café in the Village, and even wrote a song with Richie Havens.

Not surprisingly, alcohol and drug usage and "free love" were common in the Village. The first time Louis tried drugs, he became nauseated and threw up. But his uncles' example loomed largely in his mind—that a real man could party and still maintain his responsibilities. So he continued dabbling with drugs, despite the fact that cocaine and heroin made him sick. Hashish, however, became Louis's closest friend.

Wanting to pursue a career as a television actor, Louis moved to Los Angeles. He checked in at the Beverly Hills Hotel and set out to see his new hometown, driving a rented red convertible provided by Lew Wasserman and the production company. Louis put the top down and turned the radio up.

Louis encountered Hollywood's racism during his first day in town, when he was pulled over by eight separate L.A. police officers, suspicious of the young black man driving the convertible, and later that same night he was handcuffed to a tree for more than three hours, simply for exploring some of the more affluent neighborhoods in Beverly Hills after nine o'clock at night. *Welcome to Hollywood, Lou.*

His career was slow in taking hold, and Louis came close to being homeless. For a while he survived by scratching out a living as a troubadour singing folk music in L.A. coffee shops. The day the landlord was backing the truck up to his apartment ready to evict Louis, the actor received an unexpected check in the mail. Louis opened the envelope and found a check for $72,000! Richie Havens had performed Louis's song, "Handsome Johnny," at Woodstock and then put it on his album. Sales had skyrocketed but the record company did not know Louis's whereabouts so they were late in sending his royalty check. As far as Louis was concerned, the check arrived right on time.

Unfortunately, the money quickly slipped through his fingers when Louis discovered the "more sophisticated drugs," such as LSD and other hallucinogenic substances. While others reported glowing stories of rapturous experiences on LSD, Louis's initial experiences were not so positive. The first time he used LSD, somewhere in his mind a cockroach turned into a dinosaur. It scared Louis, but again the words of his father and uncles haunted him. "To be a man, you must party and still maintain your responsibilities."

Louis worked constantly in Hollywood, in both television and movies, but as soon as the director called "Cut," he retreated into isolation and loneliness. Drugs accompanied him and helped ease his mind. Resentment seethed below the surface of Louis's stoic exterior as he saw other actors receiving better parts for more money. He was convinced the reason he was passed over often related to the color of his skin. As the disease progressed in him, Louis found more reasons for failure and more excuses for his anger. Increasingly, his group of friends reflected and reinforced his perspective.

His home became known as the party place. Louis partied all weekend, but with his uncles' admonitions in his mind, he always made it to work on Monday morning, although often disheveled and groggy. Louis moved to more "natural, organic" substances that he could work out of his system through physical exercise. He tried several stints in rehabilitation centers, but kept returning to the drugs. Concerned friends tried to warn Louis, but he denied his addiction. "What are you talking about?" he responded. "I know my lines. I don't have a problem."

Even after winning an Oscar for *An Officer and a Gentleman*, little in Louis's personal life changed. During the filming, Louis was accompanied by a beautiful woman who helped ease the stress by providing him with more drugs and alcohol, and most dangerously, cocaine for freebasing. Louis got high throughout most of the movie, but thanks to working out with the Marines in preparation for his vigorous training and fight scenes, he was able to make it. He stopped using drugs near the end of filming, but went right back to his addiction as soon as the production wrapped.

As long as his addiction didn't get in the way of his work, and he could manage memorizing his lines, he continued the downward spiral. Finally, Louis hit his own bottom. He called out to God to change him. Louis entered a twelve-step program, and this time, he was ready. The treatment center did not give Louis special treatment, but helped him acknowledge his addictions. He came to realize that the resentment he harbored was unhealthy, and despite the reality of racial prejudices that he experienced, he could no longer use that as an excuse for escaping reality through substance abuse. It wasn't easy, but he turned his back on the drugs and alcohol.

Louis followed the advice of other former alcoholics and addicts and attended ninety meetings within ninety days. His relationship with God strengthened, as did his resolve to live a drug- and alcohol-free life.

He was a changed man. He was more responsible as a person, a better father, and a better professional. He cleaned up his life, showed up on time ready to work, and felt good about himself at the end of the day.

Louis encountered another life-changing experience during a trip to South Africa, where he met Nelson Mandela. Louis recalls, "I was looking out at Robben Island, where Mandela spent twenty-seven years in prison, and I burst into tears. If there was ever a man who had a reason to want revenge, Nelson Mandela had it, but he chose a path of peace. Nothing that ever happened in my life compares to what that man went through. I said, 'What am I doing? I did worse to myself than any person, white or black, ever did to me.'"

Today, Louis's life is busy helping others. "There is no such thing as impossible, no matter how far down on the scale a person might be,"

Louis tells both those who want to get clean and sober, and those who are trying to help substance abusers. He encourages people to fight the diseases of drug addiction and alcoholism through faith. "Faith is the key to freedom," says Louis. "Nothing else can take the place of God in your life," Louis told me. "Not a fancy car or a big house or all of the accolades and awards. If you are not free on the inside, you are still enslaved. But God can carry us through. The disease is with me, but my Higher Power will fight my battles for me, if I let Him." Louis is a frequent speaker to young people, cautioning them about the dangers of drugs and alcohol, as well as the pernicious and destructive attitudes fostered by racism. It was my pleasure to welcome him to share his story at one of our addiction conferences.

He has alternated between film and television ever since, and has appeared in several faith-based films, going back to the stage whenever he can. Louis maintains his transformation by continuing to attend church services or other AA or Dual Recovery Anonymous (DRA) meetings anywhere in the world where he travels, regardless of the circumstances.

For instance, Louis was in New Orleans immediately after Hurricane Katrina, trying to lend his star power to helping people in need. When he asked a taxi driver to take him to an AA meeting, the driver took him to a coffee shop in one of the seediest sections of the city. Even prior to the hurricane, this meeting location was a dangerous place.

"I'll wait here for a few minutes until you make sure you want to go in there," the driver told Louis.

Louis climbed a wrought-iron staircase and went through a large, dented metal door, where he found a tough-looking group of addicts and alcoholics. He joined them, and experienced one of the best meetings of his life.

"Everywhere in the world, the needs are the same," Louis says. "People are the same, and we all want and need a spiritual awakening that sets us free and keeps us free."

As You Believe, You Will Receive

Grandma Cartwright taught me about the Great Teacher who told a fellow who desperately needed help, "Go your way; and as you have believed, so it will be done unto you."

Think about that. As you *believe*, it will be done. That sounds great at first blush, but notice, that statement can unlock the door to success or it can imprison you in your own negative thoughts and beliefs. What you believe about yourself can help you get free or it can trap you in one dark quagmire after another. Understand, there is no such thing as an absence of belief. We all believe something, either positive or negative, so what you believe about yourself really matters—a lot.

Now here's a stunner: What you believe about yourself may or may not be true, but if you believe it strongly, that belief can set you on the path toward turning that image into a reality. S. I. Hayakawa used to refer to a self-fulfilling prophecy as a statement that is neither true nor false, but is capable of *becoming* true if it is believed. Psychologists tell us that it is an accepted truth that our minds cannot distinguish between something that is real and something that is vividly imagined. Moreover, there is a very strong connection between mind and body. What your mind harbors, your body will seek to manifest. In other words, your mind will move you in the direction of your strongly held beliefs. That's why what you believe about yourself is so important. If you believe you can never get free from drugs, alcohol, food addictions, or other compulsive behaviors, you will seal your own tomb. But on the other hand, if you can develop believable hope that you can change, your potential is practically unlimited.

QUESTIONS About BELIEVABLE HOPE

1. I developed "believable hope" because Grandmother Cartwright believed in me and instilled within me the possibilities of a better life. List three people who have modeled believable hope for you and describe briefly the good qualities you see in them:

Person: _____

Qualities: _____

_____

_____

Person: _____

Qualities: _____

_____

_____

Person: _____

Qualities: _____

_____

_____

2. On a scale of 1 to 10 (1 being "poor" and 10 being "excellent"), how would you rate your level of believable hope right now?
(Circle a number)

Poor		Not bad		Okay		Pretty good		Excellent	
1	2	3	4	5	6	7	8	9	10

In your life, what would cause this number to rise?

_____

_____

_____

_____

3. Tony Newman, Jordin Tootoo, Louis Gossett Jr., and I found ourselves powerless to manage our problems. People often feel powerless when they (place a check mark by each of the following statements that you've noticed in your life):

_____ Put themselves or others in dangerous situations.

_____ Do things while under the influence of drugs, alcohol, or food that they feel guilty about afterward.

_____ Lose respect for themselves and others.

_____ Have difficulty keeping promises.

_____ Lose control.

_____ Say hurtful or provocative statements they may not mean.

_____ Have feelings with which they can't seem to cope.

_____ Blame others for their problems.

_____ Can't see the truth about themselves.

People often feel that their lives are unmanageable when they (draw a circle around any of the following statements that describe you):

Do not follow through with planned events.

Do not manage their money well.

Use poor judgment.

Cannot function normally in everyday activities.

Are in trouble with family, friends, school, or the legal system.

Have a difficult time achieving goals.

Can't express their feelings appropriately.

Disregard personal rules, morals, or values.

Continue to use drugs, alcohol, food, or some other substance to cope with problems.

4. List five negative experiences that have happened to you as a result of addiction, depression, or substance abuse.

1. _____
2. _____
3. _____
4. _____
5. _____

5. List ten ways your life would improve if you could develop believable hope and overcome the life-controlling issues you are facing.

1. _____
2. _____
3. _____
4. _____
5. _____
6. _____
7. _____
8. _____
9. _____
10. _____

6. Tony Newman developed believable hope by asking for help from a Higher Power. What does the term "Higher Power" mean to you?

_____

_____

7. On a scale of 1 to 10, how willing are you to ask for help from your Higher Power? *(Mark a location on the scale below)*

1   2   3   4   5   6   7   8   9   10

_____

8. You are probably familiar with Reinhold Niebuhr's famous prayer, "God, grant me the serenity to accept the things I cannot change; courage to change the things I can; and the wisdom to know the difference," often

referred to as the Serenity Prayer. How might turning your problems over to a Higher Power bring more serenity to your life?

_____

_____

_____

_____

9. Which of the following character traits do you want your Higher Power to help you overcome? *(Circle all that apply to you.)*

Anger	Gossip	Vanity
Cowardice	Pessimism	Unrealistic
Self-pity	Codependence	Judgmental
Dishonesty	Hatred	Intolerance
Worry	Argumentative	Laziness
Controlling	Belligerent	Procrastination
Conceit	Inconsiderate	Rigidity
Close-mindedness	Blaming others	Selfishness
Apathy	Abusive	Prideful
Envy	Manipulative	Evasiveness
Jealousy	People-pleasing	Passive
Justifying	Lust	Petty
Self-importance	Sarcasm	Insensitive
Arrogance	Perfectionism	Know-it-all
Greed	Impatience	Defiant
Critical attitude	Insincerity	Tardy

10. Write a simple prayer, asking your Higher Power for help.

_____

_____

_____

Essential Element #2

VISUALIZE THE LIFE YOU WANT

For as he thinketh in his heart, so is he.
—*Proverbs 23:7*

Years ago, comedian Flip Wilson popularized a statement that became his signature slogan. Flip's famous phrase, "What you see is what you get!" may be more psychologically accurate than the funny man ever dreamed.

What You See Is
What You Get

Do you see yourself as attractive? Successful? Intelligent? Funny? Articulate? Winsome? Or do you see yourself as an alcoholic, a drug addict? Do you see yourself as overweight or underweight? Do you see yourself stuck in a going-nowhere job? In a dead-end relationship?

Your mindset—how you see yourself and what you believe about yourself—will make all the difference in the world in which you live.

"Come on, Michael," I hear you saying. "Do you seriously mean to tell me that changing a few thoughts and words here and there can radically alter my life?"

Absolutely. Your attitudes and thoughts exert a profound influence on how you function in life. Psychologists have discovered that human beings will move consciously or unconsciously toward that which their thoughts dwell upon, whether victory or defeat, success or failure.

> You are what you think about all day long.
>
> —*Dr. Robert Schuller*

That's why the second great truth when it comes to successful transformations is as follows: *You must specifically visualize or imagine the new world you desire to create for yourself.*

I'm convinced that the secrets of visualization were critically instrumental in my own transformation. I was only a few months sober, living out of my car, and struggling to maintain my progress, when Marshall Dowell, my good friend whom I had known from college, invited me to stay with him and his mom in Richmond, Virginia. Marshall was into the rock and roll scene, and still enjoyed partying, but he understood that I wanted to change, so he was willing to help me.

I drove to Richmond, my beat-up car breaking down several times along the way. By the time I arrived at the Dowells' home, my nerves were jangled. I was already raw from the emotion of detoxification. I felt like my body and mind were on a yo-yo, pulled constantly back and forth between my desire to use drugs or alcohol and my desperation to stay clean.

Mrs. Dowell, a kind-hearted woman with a calming spirit, must have sensed my agitation as well as my ambivalence because one day shortly after I arrived, she asked me, "Michael, have you ever read anything on Neuro-Linguistic Programming?" She showed me a book and thirty-day tape series by Anthony Robbins, and she allowed me to borrow them.

I read the book and listened to every single Robbins tape. I liked what I was learning. Anthony Robbins's material was very task oriented, and rather than processing things from the past, the focus was on where you are today, and where you want to be tomorrow. It was all about reprogramming your brain with auto-suggestions of positive thinking, visualizing the future you want, rather than merely trying to find some scapegoat or rationalization for aberrant behaviors. That appealed to me, especially since Grandma Cartwright had emphasized those things to me for years.

"Start talking to yourself differently," Anthony encouraged. "Clean up your self-talk." Robbins was also big on writing down in specific terms the life I wanted to live five years from now, ten years from now, so I began doing that. I had read similar ideas in other books, but I had never before immersed myself in the concepts. Nor had I done any of the work to bring them about in my life.

> Nothing has any power over me other than that which I give it through my conscious thoughts.
>
> —*Anthony Robbins*

The more I studied the subject of visualization, I found that most people who have succeeded in their careers, as well as their personal lives, have incorporated this sort of positive imaging along the way. People from diverse walks of life have been able to see their dreams come true, not by idly waiting for something to happen, not simply wishing on a star (or anything else), but by vigorously visualizing where they want to go and how they want to get there. And here's the secret—they have been able to see themselves living that life long before it actually happened. You, too, can create a mindset that will lead you to creating a new, self-fulfilling reality. But it does not happen by accident. It takes active, purposeful participation on your part.

I stayed with the Dowells for nearly a month, then one weekend, Marshall and a group of friends and I went to Virginia Beach. Not surprisingly, alcohol was a big part of the social scene, so I knew I had to make a decision. After the first day at the beach, I packed my bag.

"Where are you going?" Marshall asked. "What's wrong?"

"Sorry, buddy. But I just cannot be around drinking. You've been great, but I need to get back to my home group in Nashville, and get back into my AA meetings."

I didn't want to offend my friend, but I had caught a vision of the new life I wanted to create, and I didn't want to jeopardize that for anything.

Later in my recovery, I found a relationship between visualization, prayer, and meditation. I had already discovered that I could tap into a Higher Power through prayer, but it was not one-way communication. If I wanted and expected God's help, I needed to pray—to talk with Him, not in super-pious religious language, but in everyday conversation—and I also needed to listen.

"Show me the way," I'd pray, "and I'll do the work. Get me in tune with what Your plans are for my life." I faced each new decision with prayer and meditation. Almost inevitably, the answer and direction would come to me within a few days. If I would have ignored the listening aspect of prayer, however, I may have missed the message. I discovered that like a radio station already broadcasting, God was already speaking to me, and all I had to do was tune in to hear from Him.

Prayer works. And it is essential that you seek God's help when you begin visualizing the new life you want to live. We can enjoy a life of meaning, but it has to start on the inside, within us. If you don't stop and engage in prayer and meditation, you are more likely to rush through life and miss the potential that is right there in front of you.

> The creator has planted within every creature a fragment of himself, a spark, a spirit of the same nature as himself and, thanks to this spirit, every creature can become a creator. And this means that, instead of always waiting for their needs to be satisfied by some external source, human beings can work inwardly by means of their thought, their will, and their spirit to obtain the nourishing healing elements they need. This is why the teaching I bring you is of the spirit, of the creator and not of matter.
>
> —Omraam Mikhael Aivanhov

I discovered that quote in the works of Dr. Wayne Dyer, a popular communicator in the field of self-development. In his book *Wishes Fulfilled*, Dr. Dyer expresses a view of visualization consistent with mine:

> I am saying as clearly as I know how to say it. . . . *There is a plane of awareness that you can opt to live at, wherein you can, if you are willing to change your concept of yourself as an ordinary being, find yourself fulfilling any and all wishes that you have for yourself.* . . . It begins with changing your concept of yourself.[4]

That is visualization.

Wayne Dyer was greatly influenced by Neville Goddard, a popular speaker and author on metaphysical themes in the 1930s. Goddard emphasized the need to change your self-concept to elevate your life. "If you refuse to assume the responsibility of the incarnation of a new and higher concept of yourself," Goddard cautioned, "then you reject the means, the only means, whereby your redemption—that is, the attainment of your ideal—can be effected."[5]

Dyer expanded on Goddard's ideas regarding visualizing a new life: "Get this clearly in your head. . . . A higher concept of yourself involves taking on new truths and shedding your old views of what you can achieve. This is the only way you can achieve your desires."[6]

> Imagination is more important than knowledge. Knowledge is limited. Imagination encircles the world.
>
> —*Albert Einstein*

The key to effective visualization is to focus on your potential, what you can be, rather than what you currently are experiencing—where you can go, rather than the circumstances in which you presently live. These are not mere ruminations or pipe dreams. Quite the contrary, you can begin to develop in your mind a picture of the life you want to live, and amazingly, your mind will help you to bring that lifestyle to existence. When you trust your Higher Power to help you, all things are possible. Don't allow your present circumstances to deter you from what you can be.

As Neville Goddard says,

> Disregard appearances, conditions, in fact all evidence of your senses that deny the fulfillment of your desire. Rest in the assumption that you are already what you want to be, for in that determined assumption you and Infinite Being are merged in creative unity, and with your Infinite Being (God) all things are possible. God never fails.[7]

After helping people transform their lives for more than twenty years, I still get excited about motivating people to see who they can be, and the life they can live. Today, I make a living helping other people, but the truth is, I'd do it for free. In fact, for a number of years, it cost me money to work in the recovery field. But I had a passion to help people struggling with addictions and mental illnesses.

If you know *why* you are doing something, you will find a *way* to do it. That is a key to visualization as well. You need a "why" that inspires you to dream big, to see the potential that God provides for you. Most great companies and individuals start with the "why" and then they figure out the "what" and the "how."

My "why" came right out of the twelfth step in the Alcoholics Anonymous program: "Having had a spiritual awakening as the result of these steps, we tried to carry this message to alcoholics, and to practice these principles in all our affairs." That formed the basis of my motivation to help rescue people addicted as I once was. I lived with one hand up to God and the other extended to addicts, alcoholics, or mentally ill people.

One of the most meaningful achievements in my life came within a year after I began helping others. I had been sober only two years myself, but what really cranked my motor was sponsoring other people, taking people to the doctor, getting them into recovery meetings or programs, and seeing them get clean. As I helped others, I was helping myself.

Within one year of working in the field, I received an award from the National Association of Case Managers for my contributions to helping others overcome their alcoholism and drug addiction. I received the award at the organization's national convention in Chicago. No doubt, when I walked onto the platform to give my presentation in front of a thousand people in the audience, my peers wondered, *Who is this guy?* I was a newcomer to the field of case managers, treatment center directors and owners, doctors, psychologists, and psychiatrists sitting in the audience. But my "why" was so strong, I was destined to be successful.

I brought home the award and showed it to Grandmother Cartwright. She was thrilled. "You really are good at this, Michael," she said with a smile.

"You always told me to do what I love and the money will follow. I know what I love, Grandmother. I'll find a way to make some money." The positive reinforcement I received from earning that award was something that I have built upon ever since.

For your visualization to be effective, you must tap into your "why"; you must find what motivates you and gets you excited in your life. What would you do if money were not a factor? Where would you live if you had the wherewithal to do so? What would your life be like? With whom would you be sharing it?

Then as you begin to believe and see what can be, you will find yourself willing and wanting to do the hard work that will get you there, no matter what it takes.

Even Hard Cases Can Change

When the telephone rang, I wasn't surprised to hear from a prison official asking for help with an inmate. Our treatment centers had developed a reputation for excellence, even when dealing with "hard cases." Jesse Fortner, a bright young man incarcerated in his mid-twenties, was a classic illustration of a person whose condition could not be helped without addressing his addictions as well as the mental illness issues that plagued him. Most of all, Jesse needed to know that change was possible.

Growing up in a good family with caring parents, Jesse nonetheless began doing LSD with a friend in high school, and continued using various drugs throughout college. He managed to keep up appearances, as well as his grades, but on weekends, he'd party hard, attending raves where he'd take Ecstasy and other mind-altering drugs.

In his early twenties, Jesse graduated from Rollins College in Orlando, and returned to living with his family in Memphis. Before long, he was arrested several times on drug possession charges. As his self-image spiraled downward, his drug usage was building, so he used more and harder substances. He was addicted, bipolar, and, by that time, diabetic. His conduct became increasingly reckless and erratic, to the point of being delusional, high, and running around naked on the streets when the police picked him up. Because of his mental problems, the police regarded him more kindly than they may have a common criminal or drug addict. Nevertheless, they took him to jail and charged him with drug and alcohol offenses, and various other misdemeanors.

Jesse's parents were baffled. They didn't know what to do with him or how to help him. They dutifully sent him to one mental health program or drug rehabilitation program after another. But nothing proved effective.

A pattern of addiction cycles developed, including Jesse's misbehavior and his parents' enabling him. Jesse was accustomed to having his own way. And his parents loved Jesse so much they unwittingly enabled him to continue his addictions by making allowances for him and cleaning up his messes, even though Jesse repeatedly stole from them and lied to them.

All of that changed when Jesse physically struck his mother during one of her attempts to intervene in his drug-induced, self-destructive behavior. Jesse found himself back in jail again. That's when I received the phone call.

I drove to Memphis to interview Jesse, and to determine if I thought we could help him. The young man I met was disheveled and distraught, but he seemed genuinely ready to change.

Jesse had gone through thirteen other drug and alcohol programs, without succeeding in making lasting changes in his life. Each of those programs attempted to treat a part of Jesse's problem, treating him either for mental illness or for drug addiction, but never did anyone try to help Jesse by treating *both,* the addictions and mental illnesses simultaneously.

I decided to take Jesse's case.

The question of which came first, the mental illness or the drug addiction, was intriguing. The mental illness may have been lying dormant in Jesse's system, and the drugs exacerbated the situation. Mental illness doesn't always begin in childhood, and may not have shown up so overtly—or possibly Jesse could have lived a normal, healthy life with the help of some basic medications, but Jesse's use of drugs probably caused his mental illness to manifest, to play out in a more pronounced manner.

I began with Jesse as I would with most clients, helping him to honestly assess his current situation, and to build believable hope. In the process, Jesse learned about both diseases—his drug addiction and his mental illness—as though they were one. He also learned that it was safe and in his best interests to take his prescribed medications. Rather than someone forcing him to take medications, Jesse realized the value of his own medication compliance, taking his meds regularly. He also found learning about the various stages of change valuable, since that knowledge helped him feel that he was taking steps forward in a program that he could accomplish. He responded well to his counselors. He worked well with his sponsors, went to meetings, and really wanted to get clean.

I spent a lot of time with Jesse, both as a client and as a friend, partly because I wanted to help him, but also because I saw so much of myself in him. Yes, he was a disheveled, mentally ill drug addict when I had met him, but I believed he had potential to be great. I attempted to mentor him as well as to help him deal with his addictions and mental illness. Most importantly, I helped him to visualize the life he wanted to create, focusing on what he wanted to do and how he could get there. I encouraged him to write out a vision for his life, including specific goals, walking him through a plan of action, and maintaining accountability for his progress.

Jesse learned that his rehabilitation was a lifelong process, that even should he relapse, he didn't have to lose ground; it wasn't necessary for him to start over at square one. He had a strong base on which to build. Similar to an athlete who has been a champion in the past, Jesse found that a setback could be quickly overcome by putting the right steps back in place.

Jesse did so well in completing our program, eventually I hired him to help us as we helped other people with addiction and mental illness issues. He was willing to do anything he could, from answering the telephone to working in the intake program. He became so good at understanding how to help clients, I encouraged him to help counsel others.

He did, but he didn't stop there. Today, Jesse is a prominent figure for a major rehabilitation program, emceeing at conferences and serving as the spokesperson for the program. Jesse has great self-esteem, has a fulfilling job, has strong friendships, and is living the dream he visualized. In many ways, he has followed in my footsteps, so it has thrilled me to watch him succeed and help others.

Change Starts in Your Mind!

It is a known psychological truth that our lives move toward our dominating thoughts. In other words, the life on which you focus your thoughts will be the life you inevitably produce, either good or bad. So take back your life! Think on good things, things that will bring joy and love into your life. Regardless of what happened in the past, develop a new mindset today. Why rob your future by living in the past?

Dr. Wayne Dyer offers four simple rules for a healthy imagination:

Rule number one: Never place into your imagination any thought that you would not want to materialize.

Rule number two is of equal importance: Never allow your imagination to be contaminated by ideas about how your life used to be. You need faith in your power to make the nonexistent your reality. Just because you haven't experienced the magic of the nonexistent appearing in your daily life is no reason to poison your imagination with the thoughts that got you where you are now or have been for most of your life.

Rule number three: Your imagination is yours and yours alone. . . . Your imagination is your own fertile field for growing any seedlings that you choose to plant for a future harvest.

Rule number four: Do not let your imagination be restricted to the current conditions of your life . . . Your imagination is unlimited.[8]

The big question of course is: How? How can I change my thinking?

Changing your thinking is not nearly as difficult as some people purport. Instead of allowing yourself to slip into negative thought patterns, choose something positive, something good, something uplifting on which your mind can dwell. For example, most people who are trying to overcome compulsive behaviors tend to slip into thoughts such as *I can't do this. It's too hard. It's not worth the struggle.* Or *I've always been this way, and I will always be this way. Why bother?* Or *Nobody else cares whether I live or die. Why should I?*

Obviously, these kinds of negative thoughts will sabotage even the best efforts at transformation. But if you can muster the will to turn those thoughts away and think on positive things, your mind and body will work together to pull you through the darkest night or help you overcome the most difficult challenge. Try thinking and speaking aloud statements such as, "I have made some mistakes, but I can learn from them." Or "I'm a survivor. I can handle this. I've handled a lot of other difficulties." Or "I can do this. I can change. I can be better." Keep statements such as these in front of you. "I'm feeling better every day. I like the new person I am becoming." Some people find it helpful to read these kinds of statements into a recorder in their own voice and play them back to themselves every day. Hearing your own voice telling you that you can make it is a powerful encouragement.

Tape some positive phrases on your refrigerator or on the mirror where you will see them at the start of every day. Carry some cards with you on which you've written some positive statements about yourself and pull them out and review them for few minutes throughout your day. You will be amazed at how your mindset improves.

> People become really quite remarkable when they start thinking
> that they can do things. When they believe in themselves, they have
> the first secret of success.
>
> —*Norman Vincent Peale*

"Come on, Michael," I hear you wondering aloud. "You can't seri-ously expect a few simple thoughts and statements to change my life after all I've been through."

I didn't say it would be instantaneous, but by filling your mind with believable hope and visualizing the life you want for yourself, you can change for the better. And, remember, these little mindset helps are things you can do for yourself. They don't cost any money, nor do they require anyone else's involvement. This is something you can do to believe in yourself and to build upon the believable hope that you can change.

Be Positive You Can Change

"It sounds too easy, Michael."

It *is* easy, but here's the catch. Our minds have difficulty turning negative thoughts into positive actions. For example, it is almost impossible to lose weight when you keep reminding yourself how fat you are! A friend of mine who wanted to lose weight posted a mag-netic pink pig on her refrigerator door, along with the oft-quoted *Those Who Indulge Bulge!*

She later said, "I finally had to take that silly thing down. I wasn't getting any skinnier, and I noticed that my reflection in the bathroom mirror was beginning to look more and more like that pig on my refrigerator."

We move toward that which our thoughts and desires dwell upon, whether positive or negative. So remember: the second key to your personal transformation is to imagine the new world you desire for yourself; dwell on what you *want*, rather than what you don't want. If want to lose weight, begin seeing yourself as slender and healthy, rather than as "less fat." Think of how great you will look next summer in your new bathing suit. Think of how much energy you have because of the weight you have already lost *in your mind*. Let your mind dwell on pictures of you in your newly renovated form, eating healthy foods in the right quantities, exercising, and feeling good about life.

··

**Imagine the new world you
desire to create.**

··

"Mind games?" you ask. Maybe. Do they work? My friend Lauren told me that her experience attests to it.

Growing up, Lauren saw herself as a full-figured woman. Doting relatives had convinced her of this through such well-intentioned but misguided remarks as, "My, honey! You certainly are going to be a big girl! Yessir! She's a big one, she is! Big boned. Large framed. Why, I think she's going to turn out to be taller than her mother."

It just goes to show, you can't believe everything you hear—even when it comes from loving relatives. Lauren is, in fact, several inches shorter than her mother to this day. She is nowhere near being "large framed" or "big boned." She wears sizes 2 to 4, if that gives you a hint.

Nevertheless, at that point in her life, Lauren thought of herself as a large woman, and her body responded by turning those thoughts into forty pounds of excess weight. She may have continued packing on the pounds had she not dared to see herself differently.

With a bright red crayon, she wrote the number 115 on a piece of paper and taped it to her bathroom mirror, where she would see it each morning as she was getting ready for work. That was the number of pounds she wanted to be, so that was the number she let her mind dwell upon.

When Lauren's younger cousin visited and saw the reminder on the mirror, she began to laugh uncontrollably. "Is that what you think you're going to weigh?" she blurted through tears of laughter.

"That's right," Lauren replied matter-of-factly.

"But you weigh more than 160 pounds!" the cousin chuckled.

Lauren looked at herself in the mirror and resolutely replied more to herself than to her cackling cousin, "I will weigh less tomorrow."

And she did! Within six months, Lauren was down to 115 pounds, and she never regained the unnecessary weight. How did she do it? Through some specialty diet? Some expensive new workout equipment? No. By attending Weight Watchers or some other weight-loss program? Nope. As helpful as those aids may be for some people, the turning point in Lauren's life came when she began to visualize what she wanted and to "see" herself as the petite, small-framed, healthy woman that she wanted to be. Of course, she maintained a healthy diet and engaged in the most difficult type of exercise—pushing herself away from the table and closing the refrigerator door when she wanted to eat something she knew would not help her reach her goals. But the battle was won in her mind before it showed on her waistline.

"Tuning" Your Mind to What Matters

In his classic work on self-improvement and success, *The New Psycho-Cybernetics*, Dr. Maxwell Maltz emphasized that the key to changing your lifestyle is to reprogram your mental computer and establish a new mindset. He compared our minds to the homing system in a plane on autopilot. Once the destination is programmed into your biocomputer, your mindset will monitor the feedback from your destination, and make adjustments to help you reach the goal. But if your target is not specific, or if your destination is not programmed properly, your plane will wander erratically until it runs out of fuel or self-destructs. On the other hand, if you focus your mind on the life you want to create for yourself, your mind will subconsciously make the adjustments along the way to move you in the direction of your goal.

Have you ever read a book or magazine on an airplane? Most of us have. What causes you to be able to concentrate when there is so much activity around you? Simply this: Your brain filters out what you have already established as unimportant or peripheral and you focus on what matters to you at the moment. The whir of the plane's engines, or the crying baby behind you, or the banter between the young couple in front of you are barely noticeable to you because you have attuned your mind to something more important. Consequently, you don't pay attention to what is irrelevant to you. It is even possible to "tune" your mind to what matters to you, and to ignore those things that don't.

Jerry and Shirley live within twenty yards of a set of railroad tracks. When they first moved into their home, every time a train went by they felt the house shudder and the furniture shimmy, and the noise nearly scared them to death when a train roared by in the middle of the night. But within a few weeks of living there, an amazing thing happened. They no longer noticed the trains, or the shaking, or the noise. Their brains basically blocked out the irritations and the unwanted information and focused on the joy of living in the home they had purchased.

The most astounding thing happens when you begin to reprogram your own biocomputer for what you want surrounding your life. Everything unimportant begins to fade to the background. Better yet, you can actually program your mindset to seek out those things that you want in your life, while tuning out the things you do not desire. As you focus on the world you want, the world you reject becomes easier to ignore.

For instance, if you change your mindset to focus on drug-free, alcohol-free environments and friends, your biocomputer will search out people and values that are consistent with what you are seeking. Similarly, if you are programming your mindset for financial success, your subconscious will be super-sensitive to information or people who can help you achieve your goals.

If you program your mind to seek out drugs, alcohol, food, or other substances to which you know you are vulnerable, despite your declarations of sobriety or your desire to lose weight, your mindset will steer you into situations where temptation is difficult to avoid. If you want to create a transformed world for yourself, focus on what you want, where you want to go, and then allow your mindset to create the circumstances that will fulfill your desires.

Be Specific About What You Want!

The key to this sort of transformation is *specificity*. Use all of your senses to define specifically what you want your life to look like, sound like, smell like, taste and feel like. It is not enough to say, "I want a better life." Merely dreaming about living in grandeur will never get you there. You have to see it specifically, visualizing yourself there now.

> Visualize this thing you want. See it, feel it, believe in it. Make your mental blueprint and begin.
>
> —*Robert Collier*

What kind of life do you want for yourself and your loved ones? See it, feel it, describe it in as much detail as possible. When I first began to understand the potential of visualization, the mental image of my lifestyle that I wanted to create was quite grandiose, especially for someone earning a mere $16,000 per year. Nevertheless, I saw myself living in a fine house, driving a fancy car, traveling to exotic locations for vacations, and living a life free of drugs, alcohol, and mental illness.

Years later, my wife and I visualized the house in which we wanted to live. We saw it with large Southern colonial columns, with a circular driveway, a beautiful swimming pool and pond in the back, and we wrote out how each room in the house was decorated.

Understand, I saw it *before* I experienced any of it. And I have experienced everything I visualized and more. You can, too!

Your Imagination Is Powerful!

Great performers in every field have been aware of this secret for years. Athletes, astronauts, public speakers, entertainers, airplane pilots, and a variety of other professionals have long recognized the value of mental simulation and rehearsal. As we've noted, research substantiates that your subconscious mind cannot tell the difference between a real experience and a mental experience, one that is vividly imagined in your mind. In fact, it may well be that your subconscious experiences are *more* influential in controlling your performance than are your conscious experiences. This can work for you or against you.

> Our minds can shape the way a thing will be because we act according to our expectations.
>
> —*Federico Fellini*

For example, you have an important interview coming up, an encounter that could lead to a major career advancement. You do your best to prepare, reviewing the pertinent information. Yet you keep saying, "This is going to be a tough interview. I don't know if I'm good enough, or if I'm really qualified for this position. I just know I'm going to blow it."

You spend all night fretting about the interview, and the next day, as soon as you walk into the interviewer's office, your mind goes blank. A giant eraser seems to wipe clean any knowledge you ever had concerning the subjects to be discussed. The interview is a disaster. Yet fifteen minutes after the meeting, you can remember every detail of the material you wanted to present, and have come up with several perfect responses you could have given in answer to the interviewer's questions. What happened?

Basically, you visualized yourself failing. You programmed your mental computer in advance and "saw" yourself flubbing up the opportunity. Your subconscious mind, not knowing whether this was factual information or not, accepted it as truth because it was something you vividly imagined. Therefore, your subconscious mind helped you to fulfill your own prophecy.

Here is where your mindset really comes into play. Your mindset acts as a comfort zone, that area in which you comfortably see yourself performing. For this reason, it is almost impossible to consistently perform on a level higher than you see yourself. Your mindset acts like the thermostat in your home. If the temperature falls below the current setting, the thermostat will kick on the heat. If the temperature rises above the present setting, the thermostat will turn off the heat, or perhaps even turn on the air conditioning, to bring the temperature back into the comfort zone.

In a similar way, your mindset will pull you back into your comfort zone when it comes to your performance. If you perform better than you see yourself, your mindset will bring you down. If you perform more poorly than you see yourself, your mindset will pull you up.

The secret to beating this system is to visualize the new world you desire to create for yourself. Here's how you can do that. Think of your mind as a computer, with a built-in video recorder. You program the computer and you decide what images will be stored in your mental video recorder. To raise your level of performance, you must first "record" the picture of yourself doing so. You can do this by mentally seeing yourself doing well the activity you wish to do. See yourself free of alcohol or drugs. See yourself living a joy-filled life. Let your mind visualize how you will dress at the parties you are attending because you now have your weight under control.

Remember, this visualization process must be vividly imagined and *in the first person*. In other words, you must see the experience through your own eyes; it will do you little good to simply imagine yourself as a spectator would. You must sense the experience from your own inner perspective. "*I* am drug-free." "*I* am enjoying fun with my friends, without alcohol." "*I* have my gambling under control." "I am regularly taking my medications and overcoming depression." "*I* enjoy giving items to others rather than hoarding things for myself." Use the first person singular "I" to describe the life you want to live, and imagine it as though you are already living that way. "*I* enjoy eating healthy fruits and vegetables."

> Act as if you have already achieved your goal and it is yours.
>
> —*Dr. Robert Anthony*

For instance, if you want to own that beautiful, new, expensive car, vividly imagine yourself behind the wheel, expertly gliding in and out of traffic. Inhale that luscious new-car smell. Feel the wheel in your hands; see the road through your own eyes; hear the traffic zooming by you in both directions. Go ahead; blow the horn. Put on your turn signals. See yourself pulling onto the highway. Feel the surge of power as you press down on the accelerator. Smell the scent of flowers and feel the fresh air rushing against your face as you motor out into the country. Do all of this in your mind, as if you are actually driving the car.

Give no place at all to negative, counterproductive thoughts. If negative images arise in your mind as you are visualizing what you want, dismiss them immediately. How can you do that? Simple. Blink your eyes, or rub your hand across your forehead. You will be amazed how easy it is to refocus your thoughts onto something positive. Psychologists sometimes affectionately refer to this as a "mind-wipe," wiping the negative images out of your mind so that you can adjust your mental focus. Try it the next time negative thoughts or images flood your mind.

Blink. And then turn your thoughts toward the images you want in your life.

Understand, despite the plethora of stimuli surrounding us, *you* decide which picture you want to see. Then use your mental computer to visualize yourself succeeding at whatever you want to do. Concentrate on doing things right. Don't dwell on the possible obstacles or potential setbacks. Certainly you need to prepare and practice, using the techniques and information you have learned. If you visualize yourself doing something in the wrong way, you will be reinforcing your bad habits. When done correctly and repeatedly, though, your mental computer will retrieve that image and then translate it into physical actions.

To be effective, visualization requires practice, both mentally and physically. The old saying "Practice makes perfect" is not entirely true. *Perfect* practice makes perfect! But that's part of the beauty of visualization. In your mental practice, at least, you can do things perfectly; you never have to fail. You can do it right every time, assuming you are working with correct information.

Numerous stories have surfaced regarding American prisoners held captive during the Vietnam War. Some of the most fascinating accounts describe prisoners of war who had practiced golf in their minds while in captivity. Understand, they never left the Hanoi Hilton for an afternoon on the links. Yet upon their return home after the war, some of the "imaginary golfers" found that they had retained or improved their golfing abilities without actually lifting a club! They had practiced and played some of the best courses in the world—all in their minds.

Certainly sooner or later, your mindset will be put to the test in real life. Gary Anderson, former placekicker for the Pittsburgh Steelers, was consistently among the top scoring players in the National Football League and the first kicker in NFL history to have a "perfect season." In 1998, while playing for the Minnesota Vikings, Gary successfully made ninety-four out of ninety-four kicks—thirty-five field goals and fifty-nine extra points—during NFL regular season games. Only one other player in history has done anything similar. (Unfortunately, Gary missed a kick during the playoffs that year that led to an Atlanta Falcons victory over the Vikings.)

How did you do it? he was asked.

"I just made sure my foot hit the ball," Gary quipped.

Actually, Gary's outstanding success was much more involved than that. In training camp, Gary worked for hours on end, kicking field goals until his entire body throbbed from the impact of his foot blasting into the ball—again . . . and again. Gary practiced and prepared, knowing that when his opportunity in the limelight came, he had to be ready on a moment's notice.

Time after time in stressful NFL games, Gary could be seen jogging onto the field, his mind riveted on only one thing: kicking the football. "I can't worry about the pressure," Gary said when asked to describe his mindset for success. "I can't worry about the noise of the crowd or what the score is. I have to concentrate on the ball. Before I kick, all I see is the ball going through the goalposts."

And it usually did.

That is visualizing what you want, rather than what you don't want.

Here's the secret: To be effective, visualization must be *personal*; it must be *practiced*, and it must be *positive*. Again: Visualize what you *want*, not what you don't want. For some reason, your mind cannot visualize a negative command. When you stand on the tee box and address your golf ball in front of a large water hazard, you will have little success if you start out by saying to yourself, "Don't hit the ball into the water!" When you do that, your subconscious mind receives only the message, "Hit the ball into the water." If you want to avoid the water hazard, visualize something like this: "I want to loft this shot right out there on the fairway, about seventy-five yards in front of the green." Assuming your technique and information are correct, you'll have a much better chance of playing par golf when you learn to visualize your shots before swinging the clubs.

You'll find the process of visualization at work every day in success-ful businesses, colleges, and high schools. Have you ever noticed that some entrepreneurs always seem to succeed? Has it ever occurred to you that some businesses always seem to get ahead? That some schools always seem to come out on top in academics or sports? Why is that? Do they have better financial acumen, or a better human resources department, or a better recruiting program?

No, they have learned the secret of visualization. They envision their success before they begin. They dwell on what they want, not on what they don't want. They review and reward excellent work, catch-ing employees, students, or athletes doing something right; they don't waste their time complaining, chiding, or scolding about what their personnel did wrong. Certainly, errors are scrutinized meticulously to discover why and how they occurred, but once the mistake has been noted, winners place the emphasis upon reinforcing the excellent per-formances they expect.

You can do something similar. Scan back through the positive things that have happened in your life. Flip through the mental images of your successes and personal triumphs. Collect these positive images and put them in your "Success" book, either literally or figuratively. You may want to start a journal of daily successes, not a diary of "poor, poor, pitiful me notes" written to yourself. In this journal write down specific instances of your personal achievement, and all the good things you have going for you. If nothing else, it will be a tremendously inspirational book to open on a sad and dreary day, when it seems that nothing is going your way.

Whether you choose to keep a literal success book, be sure to keep a mental photograph album with the images you want to remember. Allow only the positive pictures or those negative images from which you have learned valuable lessons.

Use these images of success to help you prepare for future achievements. For example, the next time you are assigned to make a speech, allow your mind to flip back through the images of the most successful speeches you have made in the past. Refuse to dwell on the time you said something foolish or mispronounced a word. Don't allow yourself to drift back to your high school days when your teacher called your name and in your haste to get out of your chair, you ripped your slacks or skirt. Don't muse over that funny speech you thought you had made, only to discover afterward that your zipper had been down throughout your performance.

Instead, if you want to increase your confidence, scan back through some of the great speeches you have made. If you haven't made one, then make one now. You can make your speech to your spouse, or your kids, or to the baby, or if nobody else will listen, make your speech to the mirror. Concentrate on how well you have done in the past, and it will give you confidence for the task you must do today, and a well of faith from which you can draw in the future.

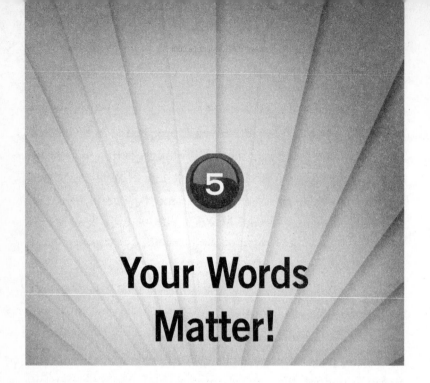

Your Words Matter!

If what we think about ourselves matters, our spoken words have an even greater impact. A friend told me an interesting story about how he learned the importance of words. He said, "When I was a little boy, if I said a curse word or lashed out maliciously, my mom would take me upstairs to the bathroom sink, pick up a bar of soap, work up a good lather, and then make me wash my lips, tongue, and mouth. You can be sure I never said those words again... at least, not within Mom's earshot. Nowadays, a mom would probably be accused of child abuse for doing such a thing, but I learned early on that words have a power of their own, and not all words are appropriate in every situation."

Our words, which can be a medium of encouragement to ourselves and to other people, are more frequently the means of diminishing or cursing them. Of course, most of us never approach people and say, "I curse you," but with our negative comments and conversations we might slice people to shreds. The wounds inflicted by words often hurt as much or more than physical blows. Many people have been verbally abused and emotionally devastated by negative statements spoken to them or about them. Worse yet, many of those searing words come out of the mouths of family members or friends.

What does all this have to do with visualization? you may be wondering. Simply this: You desperately need to understand that your words are powerful, and can be either a fountain of blessing and encouragement or cursing and death. Our words take on a life of their own. Once you have said them, whether they are positive or negative, they are out there. They never cease to exist. Your words have a longer half-life than radioactive waste, and they powerfully affect your future.

Have you ever said something that you didn't really mean? Or perhaps the words came out of your mouth sounding much harsher than you intended? Quickly, you apologize and say, "I take it back," but it is too late. Once spoken, it is impossible to retrieve our words.

That's why we need to be extremely careful in what we say not only about others but about *ourselves*.

Guard Your Words About Yourself

Ever since the Garden of Eden, human beings have been erring toward one extreme or the other regarding our opinions of ourselves. Sometimes we tend to think and speak more highly of ourselves than we should. On the other hand, too often we tend to wallow in the quagmire of low self-esteem. Because we know our own shortcomings, we loath ourselves, we think of ourselves as worthless and say awful things about ourselves. Many people confuse feeling sorry for themselves with true humility. Genuine humility is one of the grandest virtues a person can have. Unfortunately, some people have substituted an attitude of self-belittling for the positive trait of humility.

You know these people. They go around dragging themselves through the dirt, always putting themselves down by their words or actions. They live with the mistaken notion that they are being "lowly." Their motto sounds like Rodney Dangerfield's famous remark, "I don't get no respect."

You may have heard yourself making similar comments:

"I just can't stand myself."
"I'm good for nothing."
"Everything I touch I mess up."
"I am a rotten person."

The truth is, these personal put-downs are not characteristic of genuine humility. Besides being disingenuous, this sort of talk is counterproductive. Honest humility acknowledges our strengths as well as our weaknesses, our failures as well as our successes. We don't need to get puffed up over our successes; nor do we need to flagellate ourselves for our failures.

> Humility is not thinking less of yourself;
> it's thinking of yourself less.
>
> —*Rick Warren*

Avoid Negative Self-Talk

Knowing all this, why then do we continue to belittle ourselves? Stop and listen to some of the awful things you say to and about yourself.

"I'm such a jerk."

"I can never do anything right."

"If there is a way to mess up something, I'll find it."

"I'm never going to amount to anything."

"I can't stop smoking" (or drinking, or lying, or doing drugs, over-
    eating, or hoarding).

"I hate my body."

"I procrastinate all the time."

"I can't get along with other people."

"I'm never going to get my career off the ground."

All the while, your subconscious mind is right there to second your
negative motions and often add to them. "That's right," your subconscious says. "You are a poor excuse for a human being. No, you could
never do anything great. After all the horrible things you have done,
the messes you have made in your life, how could you possibly think
anything good could come to somebody like *you*?" And where did
your subconscious mind get all this ammunition? From you! By pick-
ing up on your own negative comments about yourself.

Imagine that you and your closest friend are walking down the
street together when suddenly, for no reason, your buddy begins
punching you in the stomach with all his might. Then, while you are
doubled over in pain with the wind knocked out of you, he knees you
in your nose. You fall to the ground, writhing in agony, and he begins
to kick you and jump up and down all over you.

"Wait a minute, Michael!" I hear you shouting. "With friends like
that . . ."

You are absolutely correct. Yet that is precisely what many people
do to themselves. Through their negative words about themselves,

they repeatedly beat up on themselves, and then, masochistically, keep coming back for more! They harangue themselves with all sorts of despicable and demoralizing labels.

"What a klutz I am."
"You lamebrain."
"Way to go, moron."
"Dummy! Stupid! Worthless. Atta-boy, bonehead. What a nerd you are! You gross ogre. Fat slob.
"Loser!"

Choose Your Labels Carefully

While I'm not particularly fond of labels, if you must have some, keep in mind that the labels you wear on your clothes aren't nearly as important as the labels you place upon yourself with your own words. The words you use to describe yourself will cause you to act out in the things you do.

Curt is an avid tennis player whose self-talk definitely shows up in his game. "Nice shot, wimpy!" "Keep the ball in the court, will you?" "Does your mother play? She could certainly do better than you." "You imbecile!" "Come on, jerk, can't you offer some competition?" "You limp-wristed baby!"

And these are some of the things Curt says to *himself*! No wonder he is frustrated in his game. He is talking himself right off the court. If he wants to improve his tennis, he needs to start by improving his language.

Guard your conversations about yourself, keeping your statements positive, because somebody very important is listening to every word you say. That important somebody is *you*!

Write Your Own Ticket

One day, my wife, Tina, walked into the bedroom of our ten-year-old daughter, Ally, and noticed some unusual stickers on Ally's mirror. Tina looked more closely and discovered that Ally had decorated her mirror with positive affirmations about herself. Her friend Lexi had received the stickers from her mom, and Lexi shared them with Ally. Ally picked up on them immediately.

Along with a hand-drawn heart and her name, followed by a smaller heart, Ally had applied the stickers to various locations where she can see them on her mirror each day as she gets ready for school. The stickers declare:

I am smart
I am amazing
I am strong!
Amazingly awesome
Loving
Loyal
You rock
I AM CAPABLE OF ANYTHING
I AM LOVED
I AM STRONG

Now, let me ask you: Do you think those positive affirmations will have an influence on Ally's self-esteem? Do you think the way she sees herself might influence her future?

Count on it.

Say What You Want

When you visualize yourself as you want to be, it's important to see yourself in the present, as though you are already the weight you want to be, as if you have already gotten clean and sober; see yourself free from compulsive behaviors and imagine what life without them will be, and see it as though you are living that freedom right now. Speak aloud passionately positive statements about yourself, such as the following:

"I enjoy being clean and sober."

"I am strong and healthy."

"I feel good about who I am."

"I'm in control of my body and mind."

"I am earning the respect of others."

"I am moving forward in my life."

Notice that you are declaring these things as though they are already happening. Why? Because your mind cannot tell the difference between a real or an imagined experience if you describe it vividly, passionately, and repeatedly. Your subconscious mind will simply go to work, helping you to bring those things to pass. You will begin to live not in accordance with "reality," but with your *perception* of reality.

It really matters how you see yourself, because so many of our daily decisions are not based on facts or truth, but upon information we have stored in our subconscious minds. Some of that information may be true, but much of it is based on hearsay, past experiences, the comments of friends or family members, and other input that may not always be reliable or accurate.

Who Do You Think You Are?

Like a computer responding to data that was input onto its hard drive irrespective of the content, your subconscious mind will move to meet the attitudes and beliefs you set for it, whether they are right or wrong, true or false, safe or dangerous, positive or negative. Consequently, you will probably talk, act, and react like the person you *think* you are. Psychologists have proven that you will most consistently perform in a manner that is in harmony with the image you have of yourself. Granted, even with a negative self-concept you may occasionally break out of the pattern and make that big sale, or get that promotion at work, get a date with that special man or woman, or make a sensational career move. Conversely, even people with healthy images of themselves blow it from time to time, and get down on themselves. But usually, your mind will complete the picture you tell it to paint of yourself.

If you see yourself as ugly, unlovable, inferior, or inadequate, you will act in accordance with your thoughts. You will see yourself as a loser, unlovable, and unworthy of loving anyone else.

> "I'm an alcoholic; my grandfather was an alcoholic, my dad was an alcoholic; and now I am an alcoholic, too. I can't change my family tree."
>
> "I'm depressed and I'm lonely, and that's the way my life is always going to be."
>
> "I can never do anything right."
>
> "Why me? Somebody must be out to get me."
>
> "I'll never amount to anything."
>
> "I'm just a klutz. I could never learn to dance."

No doubt, you've heard those kinds of statements; perhaps you've said them about yourself, or worse yet, *to* yourself. Your image of yourself is like a cruise control that governs your actions and performance, not permitting you to deviate from where you have set it without significant effort. All of the positive thinking, motivational messages, goal-setting seminars, and personal coaching will be useless if you continue to see yourself and describe yourself verbally or mentally as a failure.

That's why it is so important that you visualize the person you want to be and the environment in which you want to live. Remember: The person you see yourself to be in your mind will always rule your world.

QUESTIONS About VISUALIZING THE LIFE YOU WANT

1. Allow yourself to dream a little. How would your life look if you were able to implement the positive changes you desire? List three positive changes you want to see come to pass in your life:

1. _____

2. _____

3. _____

2. Imagine the life you are creating. Where are you living? What does it look like? Who is with you? What career are you enjoying?

_____

_____

_____

3. How has the way you have seen yourself in the past worked for or against your self-esteem?

_____

_____

_____

4. Where do you see yourself on the scale below?

[_____]

I'm a loser   I loathe myself   I'm an okay person   I have a lot going for me   I'm a champion

5. What are the dominant thoughts on which you have been dwelling lately? Put a plus sign or a minus sign whether your thoughts are negative or positive regarding your transformation.

_____

_____

_____

Change your self-talk by vividly visualizing yourself as the person you desire to be. Write several statements about the person you are becoming. Remember to write your statements using the first person "I" as though you are enjoying those aspects of your life today *(e.g., "I am enjoying living drug-free")*.

_____

_____

_____

_____

_____

_____

SURROUND YOURSELF WITH WINNERS

Grandma Cartwright knew an important principle in life: We become like the people with whom we most frequently associate. That is true whether those people with whom we enjoy time are positive, productive people, or individuals burdened down by addictions or other life-controlling issues. Knowing this, Grandma encouraged me to surround myself with good people. Of course, for many years, Grandma Cartwright was my best friend; she was my moral compass.

6

Stick with the Winners

You begin to create the life you want to live by changing the thoughts on which you dwell. The next important step you will take is choosing your companions. Alcoholics Anonymous displays on the walls of their meeting rooms slogans such as "Stick with the winners." These simple slogans are auto-suggestions that slip into your subconscious mind and help you to change.

In fact, one of the first slogans I saw at one of the first meetings I attended was "Stick with the winners," and one of the winners I met was Pat McDonnell, a highly successful businessman, who had also been a social-drinking alcoholic. Pat eventually became my sponsor in AA and a mentor in my life. Pat's example boosted my believable hope quotient, helping me to believe that real change was possible.

About three weeks into my new routine, I got up and dressed in an army-green workout suit and tennis shoes, and headed to downtown Nashville to an AA meeting near Vanderbilt University. During that meeting, a soft-spoken, distinguished-looking Southern gentleman named Pat, who looked to be nearly twice my age, shared a bit of his story. At the end of his brief talk, Pat made a simple comment. "I really have found a humbling point, and I feel the good Lord is giving me a chance to take a look around and find my place in life." I was intrigued by this sophisticated gentleman's admission that his addiction had brought him to the place of personal humility, and I wanted to know more.

With his quick smile and congenial features, I found it easy to introduce myself to Pat McDonnell.

"Excuse me, sir," I began. "My name is Michael Cartwright. I heard what you said. May I talk with you?"

Pat looked at me and smiled wryly at my green sweatsuit, recognizing not only our obvious age difference but also our distinctly different tastes when it came to sartorial splendor (Pat later referred to my outfit as a "frog suit"). "I'll be glad to talk with you," he said, "but you may want to find someone else here who is more your age."

"No, I would really like to talk to you," I said.

I asked Pat to tell me his story, so he shared with me how he had grown up in a strong conservative Christian home in Mobile, Alabama, yet had become involved with the local Mardi Gras cocktail party crowd, where he had made an art of social drinking. A hardworking businessman, Pat never considered himself an alcoholic, even though he had a habit of meeting the guys after work for three or four martinis, before going home to his wife and children.

Finally, his wife couldn't take it anymore. "I love you to death," she told him, "but you have to find out which way you are going."

She left. Their three sons, two of whom were already off to college and one a teenager, continued living with Pat. He was fifty years of age when his wife filed for divorce, primarily because of Pat's excessive drinking.

One night shortly thereafter, Pat walked out into the backyard and looked up toward the heavens, searching for answers. "My dad was a social drinker," he prayed, "and I've been raised going to cocktail parties, but there has to be a better way. Please help me to find it."

About a month later, a teenage friend of Pat's son Kyle was at the house, and in casual conversation said to Pat, "How are you doing, Mr. McDonnell?"

"I'm fine," Pat said automatically, but even the teenager recognized that he was hurting and the alcohol was not helping him.

"You know, Mr. McDonnell, my dad goes to Alcoholics Anonymous at 202 Twenty-third Avenue, over by Vanderbilt."

Even the thought of attending an AA meeting was repugnant to Pat. He was a mortgage banker and then a land developer who had grown wealthy building shopping centers in the Orlando area. He had always been a member of the very best country clubs. He was not about to lower himself to the level of a common drunk.

But something was drawing him inexorably toward Alcoholics Anonymous.

Almost on a whim, Pat decided to see if he could find the AA meeting in downtown Nashville. He began his search on the "other side of the tracks," expecting the meeting to be located in the industrial area, in the poorer sections of town. Pat drove up and down the streets, but couldn't find the meeting. Much to his surprise, when he finally located the AA meeting house, it was in a high-rent section of West End Nashville, in a former Vanderbilt fraternity house.

Once inside the building, Pat's surprise only increased. To his amazement, rather than a group of Bowery types, Pat recognized three doctors, four Vanderbilt professors, and a priest. "Maybe I can learn something from this group," Pat said.

For months, Pat attended the AA meetings every day at noon. He'd leave his job early from whatever part of town in which he was work-ing, often getting into the meeting just before it began. The meetings were magical for Pat. They were life to him. So he kept going. By the time I showed up, Pat was a regular and had been attending the meet-ings for more than a year.

"Okay, Michael, tell me about you," Pat said. "What are you doing?"

"I went to Middle Tennessee State University and I had a good time," I said honestly. "I just partied, so eventually, I flunked out. I went to another school, and then another, with the same results. My parents tolerated it a while, but the third school around, they said, 'No, we're not going to do that anymore. You need to find yourself.' I had been indulging in drugs and alcohol since I was a kid."

"And where are you now?" Pat asked.

I pointed out the window at a run-down, rattletrap automobile. "I'm in that car."

"What do you mean?"

"I live in that car."

When I think about what Pat did next, it still astounds me to this day. He put an arm around my shoulder—me, a drug addict and an alcoholic—and said, "Now, Mike, you can't stay in your car. Why don't you come home with me? My sons and I have lots of room, two of the boys are out of the house, and one is in school. You can stay in a spare room at our place until you get on your feet."

I could hardly believe my ears. I had just recently lost another job and been evicted from another apartment, and had exhausted all my resources. Now here was a kindly man whom I had just met inviting me into his home. What a risk that was for him!

"Oh, I wouldn't want to impose. . . ."

"No, come on home with us."

I followed Pat to his home, and he showed me an upstairs bedroom. "You can stay here till you get something else."

I had few possessions, and not many clothes, so moving into Pat's place was a relatively easy decision. Pat and his fifteen-year-old son, Kyle, made me feel right at home. They didn't seem to be worried about me being an alcoholic or an addict, but accepted me as I was, openly and generously sharing their resources with me. Pat became a role model for me. He didn't scold or preach at me; he simply modeled a different way of living. His basic message was, "If I can change, you can change!"

....

If I can change, you can change!

....

About that time, Pat was researching a building project with several doctors. One of the doctors wanted to buy into a property that Pat was developing, but Pat told him, "Look, I'd be glad to make the sale, but to tell you the truth, with the economy the way it is, that development is not a good choice for you."

The doctor thanked Pat and bowed out of the deal, but Pat had earned his trust. Later, when the same doctor wanted to do business, he called Pat again. The doctor said, "I'd like you to meet some friends of mine, some other doctors, who want to develop a wilderness program for troubled youth in Alabama."

Having been born and raised in Alabama, Pat was interested. He leased 400 acres on Lake Martin, wilderness land that had once been used by the Boy Scouts. But for some reason, the project in Alabama fell through. Nevertheless, Pat decided to develop a similar property in Tennessee. As a step of faith, he leased nearly 400 acres of wilderness property, on the contingency that he would pay for the land in full as soon as he received the contract from the state.

I watched each evening as Pat worked on a business proposal he planned to present to the state that would provide him a contract to purchase the land, build a school on the property, and create tent-area-type housing for troubled kids, as well as provide a salary for himself. I'd often ask Pat about his proposal, and he was quite generous in allowing me to read through his materials. I was intrigued by Pat's boldness in approaching the state authorities, developing a speculative idea that he felt would be a help to the underprivileged kids whose parents couldn't or wouldn't pay for them to attend such a camp. Pat put together a dynamite proposal, and the state was so impressed they gave him more than he asked for to develop the program. He hired a camp director, counselors for each group of kids staying in tents, six teachers, and a full-time nurse. Pat was simply the developer of the children's program; he hired everyone else to make it work.

Before long, Pat had nearly a hundred kids, between ten and seventeen years of age, hiking through the woods, working together, playing together, and learning positive principles and character traits such as integrity, loyalty, kindness, unselfishness, sacrifice, and other qualities for success in life that their own parents had failed to teach them. When the kids first came to the camp, many of them were one step away from juvenile prison. Most of them were undisciplined and spewed profanity. By the time they left the wilderness experience ninety days later, they were well mannered, polite, and respectfully saying things such as "Please," "Thank you," "Yes, sir," and "No, sir." I was amazed at the transformations that took place in the lives of those kids.

I stayed with Pat and his son for several months, while I attended AA meetings, worked part-time, and saved enough money to get my own apartment again. Pat never asked me for a dime; quite the contrary, he invested so much time in me, mentoring me and becoming my sponsor in Alcoholics Anonymous. We kept in touch after I moved out, but I mostly saw him at AA meetings. Nevertheless, his influence on my life, as a mentor and positive role model, has been invaluable.

Years later, when one of Pat's sons needed some help in overcoming some life-controlling issues, it was my privilege to help him get a fresh start by spending some time at one of our residential treatment centers. What goes around really does come around. It's the age-old principle that Grandma Cartwright had taught me: You reap what you sow. You get back what you give. If you plant good seeds, eventually they will reap a good harvest. Pat had sown plenty of good seeds in my life, and in addition to my family and me, many other people are still enjoying the good fruit of his efforts.

> Don't judge each day by the harvest you reap,
> but by the seeds you plant.
>
> —*Robert Louis Stevenson*

Prior to AA, most of the people with whom I hung out were doing drugs or abusing alcohol. Once I got involved in AA, 100 percent of my friends and close associates did not do drugs or drink *any* alcohol.

"Avoid negative playthings and playmates" is an essential rule when it comes to recovering from any addiction or compulsive behavior. Break off negative relationships; bad company corrupts your efforts to get free. If you are going to get serious about your transformation, the time has come for you to take action regarding the people or places that are influencing you negatively.

Make decisions about whom you will allow in your life. The truth is, there are some people you cannot be around when you are trying to get clean; you are not invulnerable even if you are in a treatment program. If you want to get free of drugs or alcohol, you must avoid other users, or addicted individuals, at least until you are strong enough to overcome temptation. If you are trying to lose weight, you must avoid individuals who say such things as "You look fine to me," or "Fat is beautiful," or who might tempt you to eat poorly, scrimp on your exercise program, or otherwise compromise your efforts.

When I was first trying to get free from alcohol and drugs, nearly all of my closest friends and family members with whom I had regular daily contact were using alcohol and drugs themselves. For me to be around them when I was trying to get clean was counterproductive. College friends who were great fun to hang out with, family members whom I loved dearly, all were dangerous for me. I had to temporarily break off my relationships with them for my own survival. Otherwise, they subtly tried to pull me back into my self-destructive patterns. "Oh, it's okay," they would say. "You can have one little drink."

"No, I can't even have one."

Pat McDonnell helped me to see the need for making a clean break in those relationships. I had to disengage from everyone around me who was using drugs or alcohol. Later, once I was clean, I could reengage them in my life, but at the beginning, I desperately needed to avoid temptation. Positively, I needed to put myself in an environment where people were not using those substances, even if it meant temporarily avoiding friends or family members.

Get the Good Stuff into Your Mind

I started reading positive books, such as Dr. Norman Vincent Peale's *The Power of Positive Thinking*, and dozens of other spiritually based books, helping me to reshape my thinking. As I read the books and considered my life, I began saying to myself, *I'm better than this. I'm living far below my potential. I can do more.* I attended motivational seminars and surrounded myself with positive influences. I watched only uplifting, inspiring, or informational television programs or movies, and when a sad, crying-in-your-beer song came on the radio, I quickly changed the station. I didn't want anything to interfere with the new mindset I was visualizing for myself. I began to see myself as successful, rather than constantly struggling to make ends meet; healthy rather than addicted; free to do anything I put my mind to doing. Most importantly, I specifically visualized the kind of life I wanted to live. And I had some grandiose ideas about what that life might look like. I imagined myself enjoying that life, even before it became a tangible reality.

I visualized the house in which I wanted to live long before I ever had anywhere near enough money to buy a shack, much less a mansion!

There's No Shame in Mental Illness

Getting off the prescription drugs took longer. I found an excellent doctor in Nashville who helped me to titrate off the medications. This did not happen overnight. I continued to struggle with mental illness for several years, so I remained on antipsychotic and antidepressant medications for the first few years of my recovery. During that time, I read everything I could find on mental illness to learn about my disease. I spent hours in the Vanderbilt University library, studying every article I could find on the subject of dual diagnosis and co-occurring disorders, drug addiction, alcoholism, and depression. I discovered that great men and women down through history had battled with depression. Abraham Lincoln, for example, struggled with depression most of his life, as did one of the greatest preachers the world has ever known, Charles Haddon Spurgeon. Winston Churchill's proneness to depression haunted him his entire career. But such mental illnesses do not have to define you or your future.

Ironically, as a little boy, I used to pray for mentally ill individuals almost daily. Now, I was the one asking God for help with my mental illness.

It took me several years and a lot of hard work to get back to my physical, emotional, and mental baseline. I refused to feel sorry for myself. Moreover, I discovered the fallacy in accepting without question the opinions of the medical community. For instance, I was told that I would be on psychotropic drugs for the remainder of my life, that I would never be able to hold down a real job, that I would be unable to work or go to school. The doctors recommended that I go to vocational rehabilitation, a training center where I could pass the time, where I might be able to be retrained to function in some sort of menial job. I challenged that sort of medical advice every time I received it.

I "fired" several psychiatrists who didn't understand cyclic psychosis well. I interviewed psychiatrists as though I were hiring them for a job. Most doctors are wonderful, but some, especially neurologists and psychiatrists, can come across as though they are doing you a favor by treating you. "You don't understand," I told several doctors. "I'm paying you; you are not paying me. You are working for me."

I had researched my mental illness and figured that if the psychiatrist didn't know as much about the subject as I did, it was silly to go to him or her. Eventually, I found a fabulous psychiatrist who understood the challenges I was facing.

Had I not taken responsibility for my own wellness, I could easily have been relegated to taking more medication, living life in a drug-induced haze. I would have been stuck in the system, attempting to cope with my existence. Thank goodness for a doctor who not only helped me medically, but motivated me to get well and stay well.

One of the proudest moments in my life was giving a keynote speech to the Tennessee Alliance for the Mentally Ill, sharing my experience of overcoming mental illness. I told how I had overcome cyclic psychosis and schizophrenia and was now a fully functioning member of society and helping others. Although I had once been a homeless alcoholic and drug addict, it took a bigger leap to get over the mental illness. Using drugs or alcohol was my choice; mental illness was something I had inherited, but I refused to allow it to define me. The crowd understood and responded with a rousing, prolonged standing ovation.

It takes a lot of work to get free of medications—it certainly did for me—and you may need therapy, a competent medical team, and counselors who can help you get off those legal drugs. In fact, the process of slowly tapering off the medications took a lot of time and patience, but I finally conquered the need for even prescription antidepressant drugs.

It wasn't easy. No question about it: It's tough getting clean and staying clean. But if you remain committed, work with your doctors or therapists, regularly attend meetings or other events where you receive inspiration and positive peer pressure, avoid negative influences, surround yourself with people who will lift you up and encourage you rather than make excuses for you or pull you down, it is entirely possible to live free of addictions.

Tell Somebody!

Do you remember the activity in elementary school called "Show and Tell"? We'd bring some item to school and at some point the teacher would ask us to show the item to the class and tell all about it. In a similar way, if you want to break off with one way of life and begin a new pattern, you must *tell* and *show*. Tell your family, friends, and associates what you plan to do, and then show them that you are doing it. It's irrelevant whether they believe you or not. The person upon whom your words will make the most profound impression is *you*! There's a power released by the mere speaking out of your words, declaring your freedom from drugs, alcohol, or other compulsive behaviors. Just hearing yourself say those words, "I'm clean; I'm living differently than I have in the past," does something positive for you. Those words get down into your subconscious mind, and you begin to believe in yourself.

Second, when you tell someone else, or a bunch of people, that you intend to live differently, you can be sure they are going to watch you, to see if you are as good as your word, or if you are just blowing hot air. Whether you want it or not, there's an element of accountability that results when you tell someone else that you plan to change, an accountability that you may not have if you keep your new commitment to yourself. The knowledge that someone else is looking over your shoulder, keeping an eye on you, can be an incentive to do the right, healthy, liberating things that will keep you on track.

Even if your first steps in the right direction are baby steps, they are incredibly significant. Dare to step forward. Otherwise, all your words about a fresh commitment are mere puffs of air. Words without actions are meaningless when it comes to forming new habits. It takes concentration and effort to pull off a life transformation.

One of the first things I did after deciding to get clean was to tell all my friends, many of whom used drugs and alcohol regularly, that I was making a change. "I'm quitting," I said bluntly. "I'm done. I won't be able to hang out with you anymore. I'm getting away from all this." Then I showed them that I was serious by faithfully attending Alcoholics Anonymous meetings.

Convincing my friends that I was serious, that I truly wanted to change, and was committed to change was another matter. None of them overtly tried to sabotage my efforts, but they had known me for so long as a drug user and an alcoholic, the idea of me being rehabilitated was a difficult concept to get through their heads. They'd often say, "Come on, Michael. Let's go have a few beers."

They weren't being rude or rotten. They were offering me what they had, and I appreciated it, but I knew that what they had could be devastatingly destructive to me, so I slowly came to the conclusion that I could no longer risk being around my friends who were still using drugs or abusing alcohol. I couldn't hang out with them; I couldn't go to parties with them. I didn't make a big deal about it. I just tried to avoid them as much as possible. Inevitably, though, I'd bump into someone who knew me as Michael the party guy.

"Hey, Michael, where have you been?"

Sometimes I tried to explain, but more often I'd simply say, "Oh, I've just been working on something." The road less traveled is a much more difficult path than going the way of the crowd or the way you've always traveled.

I got in the habit of saying things such as, "I'm trying to get clean and I just can't be around you. Sorry, man; I have to leave."

And I did.

Help Someone Else

Gratitude is one of the great motivators in life—or it should be. Once you find freedom yourself, find someone else that you can help. You don't need to wait till you know all the answers; you may not even know all the right questions. That's okay. Part of your own continued healing will be your willingness to share what you have received.

Grandma Cartwright had always taught me, *Get out of yourself. Do something to help someone else, and you will feel better as well.*

Now that I was off drugs and alcohol, I wanted to help other people get clean.

I always enjoyed working in sales. Grandma had encouraged me along that line and so had others. But shortly after I got clean, a case worker approached me and said, "You ought to be doing *this* job."

"What are you talking about?" I hedged. "I'm still struggling myself."

"No, you're doing great. How long have you been clean now?"

"About two years."

"That's perfect. You're far enough along the way that you know what it's like to be free, but you're not so far removed that you can't remember what it feels like to be addicted and hopeless. You have a job now, and you are so much more functional. You ought to be helping others by this point."

I had read and studied a number of books about addictions, and I had enrolled in Nashville's Trevecca University to learn more. As I studied, I was shocked to discover that approximately 22 million Americans regularly abuse alcohol or drugs. National surveys indicated that more than 65 percent of U.S. families are affected by drug or alcohol abuse, yet despite the prevalence of substance abuse, many who are addicted or affected by an addicted person are unable to recognize the symptoms or understand the importance of treatment until the problem is in advanced stages.

Think about that. Whether because of denial, embarrassment, ignorance, or some other reason, such naïveté would be tantamount to millions of people living atop Mount St. Helens or some other volcanic location, with an ever increasingly seething cauldron of pressure building, *building, BUILDING*—about to blow life apart with unprecedented personal destruction—yet people are going on their way, oblivious to the impending disaster.

Common Critical Factors of Addiction

What causes people to adopt addictive lifestyles? Nobody in his or her right mind prefers to act in self-destructive patterns. They have gotten there somehow, but they probably never made a conscious choice to do so. Yet, until the twentieth century, that was the prevailing theory regarding addictions—that people willingly chose to use drugs, alcohol, or other life-controlling substances most likely because of their own moral failings or weaknesses. It was thought that if someone once chose to indulge in such behavior, merely by stopping the behavior, the person's life would be transformed. Unfortunately, for many people, that theory did not bring satisfactory results.

Others argued that alcoholism and drug addiction, as well as other compulsive behaviors, were simply matters of biology. "It's in your genes," became the reason that some people are more susceptible to addictions, so not surprisingly, people in this camp regard an addiction as a disease.

More recently, the "social learning model" has come into vogue among therapists helping addicted individuals. This theory emphasizes learned behavior. The explanation for using dangerous substances is simple: they temporarily make people feel good. Since a person likes the way the substance makes him or her feel, the behaviors are reinforced. By the time significant negative consequences occur as a result of the behavior, a strong psychological and physical addiction has already developed.

Why? Mental illness. Trauma. Pain. It could be any of a variety of reasons that leads a person to seek relief through alcohol or drugs or food. Additionally, most people with mental illness want to alleviate that pain. They think they can do so through drugs or alcohol or food, never expecting to become controlled by the very substances that are bringing them such temporary pleasure. Other people become involved in "process" addictions—addictions such as gambling, sex, Internet porn, hoarding, or video gaming.

Regardless of how a person came to his or her addiction, the question remains the same: How can we turn on the light switch that will lead the person to seek help? More often than not, the answer is to move forward, the person must simply let go.

Three Inevitable Elements of Addictive Behavior

How do you know when someone is addicted or needs help to overcome negative, life-controlling issues or behaviors? You will most likely discover three common elements:

1. *Compulsion.* "I have to have it. I must do it," the person claims. Sometimes not even a concern for dying will keep a person from indulging in his or her addiction. Indeed, many addicted individuals almost *want* to die. Have you ever visited a hospital

and noticed the number of patients hooked up to intravenous machines dispensing medications into their systems, yet the patients are outside smoking cigarettes? They have given up hope of ever being free of their addictions.

2. *Inability to quit.* "I've tried before and just can't stop."

3. *Negative consequences.* These include collateral damage in the lives of others; the addiction is spilling over into the lives of other people.

Some people cannot handle adversity, so they slip into addictive lifestyles. Others cannot handle their own success, and may feel guilty or unworthy of it. They plunge headlong into self-destructive activities, almost as if saying, "If the rest of the world can't see how unqualified I am for this level of success, allow me to show you my inadequacies." They will do things that put themselves in positions to fail rather than to succeed, and when they are found out—which almost everyone is in these days of instant communication—they recoil in horror that anyone could suggest such a thing about them.

Two Surprising Causes of Addictions

Studies in behavioral health continue to find that previous trauma often leads to addictive behaviors. One of our research studies discovered that 76 percent of the people who came to us for help had experienced a head trauma of some sort, either through an accident or abuse.

Besides the trauma itself, too often, the medications used for treating head traumas are highly addictive, equally as dangerous as heroin and other street drugs. If a patient is not carefully monitored, and weaned off of pain medications and antiseizure medicines as soon as possible, such medications can have devastating long-term ramifications.

Sexual or other physical abuse earlier in life is another major cause of life-challenging addictions or compulsive behaviors. Sandra LeSourd, a former beauty queen and Walt Disney artist, admitted, "My earliest addiction was for love and approval."[9] As a five-year-old, her willingness to passively comply with the requests or demands of the adults in her life led to a relative sexually abusing her. Sandra's guilt and confusion over being sexually molested as a child resulted in years of substance abuse, including prescription medications, alcohol, and drug abuse as an adult.

Emotional trauma because of abuse may lie dormant for years, and then suddenly reap a horrible harvest. Physical beatings during childhood, verbal abuse, emotional abuse, and of course, sexual abuse often lead to addictive behaviors. It is difficult to generalize here. What might affect one person negatively may not affect another at all. Others might respond to those negative influences by becoming promiscuous, while still others may respond by becoming sexually cold or inhibited. Many turn to drugs, alcohol, or food to escape their pain, whether present or past, and even fear of pain in the future.

Oprah Winfrey is one of the most successful women in the world, yet she has struggled with weight issues again and again. She has acknowledged being sexually abused as a child, and it may well be that those experiences influence her to this day.

I can relate. I was abused emotionally and sexually as a child, and that no doubt had an influence on me becoming addicted to drugs and alcohol.

My cousin Billy was both my hero and my nemesis. I was ten years old and Billy was sixteen, so, of course, I looked up to him and loved him. Billy was popular with all the neighborhood guys, and even more popular with the girls. Yet for nearly three years, Billy took special pleasure in torturing me in every way that he could—physically, mentally, sexually, and emotionally.

Neither Billy's parents nor mine had any idea how he abused me. Around adults he turned on the charm and seemed like a normal kid. But when he babysat me, he was a psychopathic terror. He let me drink, smoke cigarettes, and get high, but he also would shoot me in the head with a BB gun. One day he shot me in the arm with a cinnamon toothpick, just to see how it might affect me. Sometimes he set me up to fight with other kids my age, just for kicks. He was also the one who bought the pot that we smoked. Billy was a big part of accelerating my downward slide during my teenage years. I didn't fully understand that what he was doing was wrong; it was simply part of life that I accepted.

Even our painful or embarrassing experiences can be turned around and used for good if we will allow our Higher Power to help us do so. Because of the abuse I was made to endure by Billy, I developed a compassion and an empathy for people who have suffered physical abuse, recognizing that what they endured because of someone else may help explain their struggles today.

Pushing Through New Doors

Years later, I went to the Mental Health Cooperative (MHC), a community mental health center serving addicts and alcoholics in some of the tougher sections of Nashville, and I applied for a job as a case worker, working with low-income, inner-city people. Amazingly, I was hired. That step helped me more than any help I could ever offer to them. Getting out of myself, helping another person, as Grandma put it, helped me to get my eyes off me.

Working with some of those inner-city addicts and alcoholics became one of the most rewarding experiences of my life. I could relate to them, and they related to me. I treated every person as though he or she was my best friend. Most responded positively. One person I met at the Mental Health Cooperative especially captured my interest. And she was definitely not a client.

7

Good Friends and Partners Matter

Once I made a clean start, I decided that I wanted to follow Grandma's instructions and surround myself with positive people, people who would inspire me to be better rather than being a drag on my spirit. The first day on my new job, the boss informed me that I would have to undergo training before being permitted to handle clients' cases. That made sense to me, and I was excited to get started. I was even more enthusiastic when I walked in to my first training session and met my trainer, Tina Fisher.

She was beautiful, and she was bright and articulate, with a keen sense of humor and lips that turned quickly to a smile. But her most endearing quality was one that I didn't perceive at first brush: Tina had a heart of compassion and a desire to help people who were hurting. She was perfect.

Dressed in a sophisticated-looking business suit, Tina presented herself as the quintessential professional. As much as I was attracted to her, she was assigned to train me to help the clients coming to MHC, so I did my best to maintain a respectable decorum. She was, after all, the key person who would either open or close the doors to my future with the company. She spoke kindly, yet seemed cool and unimpressed with me as she patiently walked me through my responsibilities as an MHC case worker. Satisfied at last that I understood the job and the MHC approach to helping people struggling with substance abuse, she passed me. I was officially now a Mental Health Cooperative case worker.

Tina and I didn't interact a great deal since her work cubicle in the large office was on the other side of the building. Occasionally, I'd see her, however, and we always exchanged friendly greetings. She'd ask me how work was going, how I liked the new job, and that sort of thing, but our conversations rarely went beyond platonic subjects.

After working at MHC for nearly a year, I began talking about the possibility of opening my own halfway house for alcoholics and drug addicts who were also struggling with mental health issues. Anna, one of my coworkers, was intrigued by my ideas. "You ought to talk with Tina Fisher," she suggested. "It sounds to me as though you both are trying to do something similar."

"Really?" My interest was instantly piqued. I liked imagining that the attractive trainer and I were on the same wavelength. "What do you mean?" I asked Anna.

"Well, Tina is trying to save an apartment complex from being torn down on Music Row. It's an older property being used to house clients with mental illness, and somebody wants to purchase it and turn the property into an office building. All I know is that Tina's clients have been in that house for quite a while, and she is doing everything possible to keep them there. Sounds a lot like what you want to do by opening a halfway house. You two ought to team up and talk."

I thanked Anna and looked for an opportunity to broach the subject with Ms. Fisher. One day I saw Tina, and I asked her about her efforts to save the Music Row halfway house.

"They are giving us quite a runaround," she said with a sigh, "since we don't have nonprofit status there. I want to write a grant request, but everyone says we need a 501(c)(3) organization to do it, and that is complicated."

"Oh, really? That's not so hard. I can help you with that." I had never before set up a tax-exempt organization, but my friend Pat McDonnell had successfully set up a nonprofit organization for the children's camps, and I had read his material and quizzed him all about it. I knew I could do it—and Tina was quite attractive!

We agreed to get together to talk further, so one night we stayed after work and discussed the project. During that meeting, I proffered, "Hey, I have two tickets to a Vince Gill and Amy Grant concert coming up this weekend. Would you like to join me? We can talk more about the project."

"Well, yes, I'd love to go," Tina said.

I picked up Tina in my dumpy, $2,000, blue Toyota Celica. Miracle of miracles, she consented to get into the car! As we drove to the concert, Tina looked over at me and said, "Now, what's the deal here? Are we on a date, or are we just working? What's going on here?"

I did my best to sound laid back and cool. "I thought we were meeting to talk about the project, and I just happened to have these two concert tickets. Besides, from what I understand," I ventured, "you already have a boyfriend. And I wouldn't want to interfere with that. That wouldn't be right, and I won't do that."

She looked at me and smiled. "Yes, that's true. I have been seeing someone, but that relationship isn't working out too well." She turned her head and looked out the window, so I let the matter drop.

We went to the concert and had a great time together. That night, after I got back home to Pat's place where I was still living, Tina called me. "I called him and told him, 'It's over; I can't see you anymore.' So let's go out."

"What?"

"My boyfriend. I told him it is over."

What I didn't know at the time, Tina had also told her best friend that night, "I've met the guy I'm going to marry. He just doesn't know it yet."

A few days later, I said something almost identical to one of my best friends: "I met this girl, and I know she is the one for me." Tina and I had discovered something special. Within three weeks' time, we were discussing marriage.

I took Tina to meet my grandmother, and we went out to dinner together. Grandma suggested that the portions served by the restaurant were so large the women could almost share one meal. "That's a great idea!" Tina agreed. "I'll split that with you. As a matter of fact, I think I have a coupon here that will reduce the price even further."

A coupon? Grandma looked at Tina with absolute adoration. Finally, I was with a woman who understood the value of a dollar and was concerned about frugality! Grandmother was thrilled. Tina was indeed a good money manager. She was also a hard worker who had held down three jobs to buy her own condo and her own car. She was just Grandma's type, which, of course, meant she was also perfect for me.

After we had dated for about a year, I contrived a fabulous strategy for asking Tina to marry me. I had saved money for months and had a ring made especially for Tina. I took her out to eat at a nice restaurant. The entire way there, Tina complained about spending so much money. When I finally had an opportunity, I had her close her eyes, and I got down on my knees as I slipped the ring on her finger. "What in the world are you doing?" she asked. She thought I was just fooling around. But I wasn't.

"I'm asking you to marry me," I said, "if you'll give me a moment here."

She gave me much more than a moment.

We were engaged for another year as we saved money for our wedding. We were married at the Grand Lido Hotel overlooking Negril beach in Jamaica on October 5, 1996. Tina not only became my wife; she became my primary partner in life, my soulmate, my best friend. She believed in me, and she believed in my dreams when nobody else was willing to give me a chance.

8

A New Way of Considering Change

In 1996 I went back to college at night to complete my bachelor's degree with Tina's blessing. She supported us and I helped as best I could, but mostly I studied like a man obsessed with gathering knowledge—which indeed I was. For nearly a year, I read everything relevant to my field that I could get my hands on, as I worked around the clock to finish my thesis—an eighty-page research paper on dual diagnosis. In the course of my studies, I continually encountered the names of Dr. Carlo DiClemente and Dr. James Prochaska, research psychologists whose work on the Stages of Change—the common steps most people encounter as they decide whether change is worth it—had become a standard model in recovery work. I also was intrigued by the work of Dr. Ken Minkoff, an expert on integrated treatment of individuals with co-occurring psychiatric and substance disorders. Minkoff's work on "value-driven" change, seeing change as starting in a person's heart and attitude, especially piqued my interest. Dr. Minkoff was speaking my language!

I was fascinated as well by the works of Dr. Bert Pepper, who had taught at Harvard and New York University on addiction, alcoholism, and mental disorders; and Dr. Bill Miller's theories of "motivational interviewing," how it is possible to motivate people to change. I culled truth and techniques from these well-established experts and gradually formed my own methods and philosophy. At addiction conferences, I sought out these experts, wanting to learn from them. Dr. Bill Miller's motivational interviewing techniques especially resonated with me, since one of my passions was to encourage people rather than condemn them for their behavior, to pump them up rather than excoriate them and put them down. I wanted to get people excited about recovery, and to let them know that change was possible. I knew from my own experience that what they really needed was believable hope.

When I began having conferences of my own, one of the first experts I invited to speak was Dr. Carlo DiClemente. By that time I was quite familiar with his work and writings, and DiClemente's practical, workable stages of change were welcomed by the substance abuse and mental health workers in attendance. Later, I invited Ken Minkoff, Bert Pepper, and Bill Miller to speak at our conferences as well. I learned from all of these experts, synthesizing the best of their work into my own practices for mental health as well as the best techniques in dealing with substance abuse.

The Six Stages of Change

DiClemente and Prochaska suggested six stages involved in making any change, but especially the change involved in overcoming addictive or compulsive behaviors. These six stages sometimes overlap, and people who are trying to transform their lives often cycle back through various stages of change before they achieve their goals. In fact, if you are considering a transformation in your life, rather than thinking of these stages as a linear progression, in which a person moves along a straight path, it is more helpful to think of the change process as though you were climbing a spiral staircase. While there may be days when you feel as though you are standing still, and haven't made any progress at all, or worse yet, have fallen back a few steps, it is important to remember that you are still higher on the spiral than when you started on the path to change.

Imagine with me that you are considering a major change in your life, whether you want to get off drugs, stop drinking, or get your weight under control. Without getting bogged down in the deep psychological details of the doctors' study, let's consider how these stages of change work in your life or in the life of somebody whom you are trying to help.

Stage One—Precontemplation

The person in precontemplation has not yet considered the need for personal change. He or she is in a "pre-believable hope" stage. He doesn't believe that he can live a day without alcohol or hope that life can be better by not drinking; she cannot even consider her life apart from the drugs she keeps ingesting.

The person in this stage is often living in denial and doesn't recognize that a problem exists. He or she doesn't have a problem, of course;

it is *everyone else* who has the problem! Others around the person may be encouraging him or her to seek professional help, or may be reminding the person of the need for change, but the affected individual isn't convinced.

He or she may sound something like this:

> "I wish you guys would just mind your own business and leave me alone. I'm fine the way I am."
>
> "I don't have a drinking problem. I can stop drinking [or doing drugs, etc.] any time I want to. I just don't want to right now."
>
> "Hey, I'm not the one with the problem here. You might have a problem, but I'm fine."

When I began personally working with clients who had addictions or engaged in compulsive behaviors, I noticed people in the precontemplative stage often resorted to "The Four Rs"—reluctant, rebellious, resigned, or rationalizing.

The *reluctant* person says, "I haven't done anything wrong; I don't need to change. I'm not hurting anyone. It's my life; it's my body; I can do what I want."

The *rebellious* person frequently lashes out at others for exposing the need for change. Teenagers, for example, often fall into this category as they rebel against parental authority. Adults with controlling issues can be rebellious as well. "Don't tell me what to do. You don't own me"; or "You have no right to tell me what I should do. Who do you think you are?"; or "This is my way of dealing with life, so don't think I'm going to stop. I'm having too much fun." The rebellious person may seek to blame others: "They are the ones with the real issues, not me. They just need to mind their own business!"

The *resigned* person has given up, sometimes even without a fight.

He or she has accepted the inevitable. "I've tried before and failed. What's the use in going through another program? All they want is my money"; or "This is who I am. I'm a food addict. Always have been and always will be. There's nothing I can do about it. I just have bad genes."

The person given to *rationalization* wants you and everyone else to believe that his or her destructive behavior is not so bad, and even has benefits. "Hey, I'm a musician, so I need that high for my creative juices to flow"; or "You may not understand this, but I can drive better with no sleep and a few pills"; or "Oh, don't worry about me. I only use cocaine on weekends. It's my party drug of choice and it helps me unwind."

But I Don't Like Change

When you think about making changes in your life, the prospect may scare you, or it may seem intrusive to you. You may have grown comfortable with your life the way it is, even if it includes some elements that you know are destructive. Some people say that change is inevitable, and the only sure thing in life is change. But that isn't good news for someone in a precontemplative state. He or she cringes even at the thought of changing. Others stonewall against it as long as possible.

Nevertheless, you will discover that once you decide that you want to improve your life, each step along the way is more rewarding. It may not always be easy, but it is worth it. If you (or someone you are trying to help) can list some positive changes that might improve life, the benefits of changing may become self-evident. Imagine how good you might feel if you:

Stopped smoking

Got your weight under control

Began to lead a sober, drug-free, clean lifestyle

Could control your temper

Had all the money in a savings account that you have gambled away

Didn't feel compelled to hang on to every item in your possession

Enjoyed a fulfilling job in a career you felt mattered

Had a healthy and happy sexual relationship

Could pay your bills without worrying about a check bouncing

Were able to enjoy spending time with your family

As you think on these things, if something stirs within you that says, "Yes! That's what I want," you may be ready to move into the next stage of change.

What Should I Do?

One of the best things you can do when you begin to feel motivated to change is to contact a professional who can help you. That's what my life is all about, so please take advantage of the resources I've given you in the back of this book. There is no obligation, and you have nothing to lose by contacting us. But whether you choose to contact me or someone else, make sure that person is willing to talk with you honestly and you are able to trust him or her. Choose someone who will understand what you are going through, so you can build believable hope, rather than merely talking with someone who wants to try to "fix" you.

A second important step will be to educate yourself about whether your situation could be a life-controlling challenge, and to identify the real problem with which you are dealing, as well as the possible solutions and places you can find help. Books, audiovisual materials, and helpful Internet downloads abound nowadays for nearly every ailment in life.

Third, make a list of the differences between how you view yourself, and what others—especially people who are willing to be honest with you—tell you about yourself. Your spouse or parents may be able to do this, or a pastor, a competent counselor, or sometimes even a judge. But get the truth.

Fourth, consider your choices. Draw a line on a large piece of paper and on one side list those things that might happen if you don't change, and on the other side, list what might happen if you do. If you continue on the path you are currently traveling, will you lose your marriage? Your children? Your job? Will you go to prison? Will you die of heart disease, contract diabetes, overdose on drugs, or develop some other debilitating condition? Will you remain in a no-win situation? What consequences are likely if you do not change?

> If nothing changes, nothing changes.
>
> —*Bumper sticker*

On the other side of the line on your paper, list some things that might happen if you do change. For instance, you may live longer; you may live healthier, happier, and more prosperously; you may feel better; you may keep your job and even get a better one; you may enjoy an improved relationship with your loved one; you may save more money; you might be able to enjoy a more comfortable lifestyle.

As you consider the things holding you back from change, ask yourself honestly, *Are these things worth the pain and insecurity I may experience by engaging change in my life?*

If you feel that change may be worth considering, you are ready to move into the next stage.

Stage Two—Contemplation

When you begin considering the possibility of making a change, even if you are still uncertain, fearful, or undecided whether you really want to take that step, you will be in the contemplation stage. But now you at least have a measure of believable hope that change is possible. That's not to say that you will be totally convinced that change is desirable, or even in your best interests (or the best interests of the person for whom you are attempting to help clarify these issues), but you are now at least aware of a problem and willing to think about it—to kick the tires, so to speak—and explore how transformation might work for you.

In this stage, ambivalence is common. *Ambivalence* regarding change is that back-and-forth feeling between attraction and repulsion: "I want to change. . . . I don't want to change. Change is good; no, I hate change!"

A person in the contemplation stage may say things such as

"I'm sick of all the consequences of my addiction, but I'm scared I won't be able to stop."

"Sometimes I feel like changing; at other times, I don't."

"Hey, I'm not promising anything. But I'll think about it."

"I've heard there is help for someone like me, but I'm not sure where to find it."

"The thoughts of change scare me, but remaining the way I am isn't exactly comforting either."

Often, the greatest inhibitor to change is fear—fear of the unknown. "What's it going to be like?" or "People may not like me if I change."

Fear of embarrassment or letting someone down sometimes stifles a person's willingness to consider change, too.

It's important to understand that fear of change is normal. Almost everyone experiences those kinds of fears to some extent. Some fears are actually helpful; they help us avoid danger and overcome life-threatening situations, and can even kick us into survival mode when necessary. But most of our fears are futile or foolish; in truth, relatively few of our fears are based on fact and even fewer are worth worrying about. The things that seem most menacing in our imaginations rarely come to pass, especially when you are willing to face your fears head-on. Eleanor Roosevelt said, "You gain strength, courage, and confidence by every experience in which you really stop to look fear in the face. You must do the thing you think you cannot do."

If you are contemplating a change, try to open your mind to both the positives and the negatives that such a change will produce in your life. While transformation certainly has its benefits, you may choose the tried and true, familiarity over the risk of something new. That's not unusual for someone in the contemplative stage. But be honest: What are your main concerns about your present lifestyle or situation? What will your life be like if you *don't* change? Is that what you really want? What do you want your life to be like one year from now? List a few advantages or benefits of making some changes in your life. And here's the big question: Do you believe it is possible for someone like you to overcome the behavior or attitudes that have brought you to this point? In other words, have you discovered believable hope?

The contemplation stage is the time to begin visualizing the life you've always wanted. What does it look like, feel like? Who is there with you, and what is your lifestyle? Consider your addictions (or, better yet, your lack of them), your mindset, your appearance, your friends and family, your romantic relationship, career, and recreational activities. What would you really want life to be? Go ahead; dream big!

Consider the Pros and Cons of Change

Again, draw a line down the middle of a piece of paper. On the left side of the line, list some reasons that you want to change. Then on the right side of the paper, list the reasons that you don't want to change, or some possible consequences of not changing. Now, look over your lists and circle the reasons that are most important to you. If you find that your strongest reasons are on the change side, you are ready to get started.

Stage Three—Preparation

Okay, you have decided to make the change and you are motivated to do so. Now it is time to start asking the question: How can I really do this? How can I make a lasting change in my life that truly transforms my actions as well as my attitudes? It is in this stage that you begin to not simply visualize what your life could be if you were free from substance abuse or other constraints, but to surround yourself with winners who can help you achieve your goals. Now it's time to put yourself in a position to succeed. As you begin thinking in these terms, you'll find that you have some serious decisions to make as you lay out your game plan. Most people in the preparation stage don't start by immediately developing a step-by-step process to change. Rather, they often begin simply by acknowledging what might be obvious to people around them.

The person preparing to change may say things such as:

"I really want to stop overeating, but I enjoy food so much, I'm not sure I can do it."

"I'm determined to get help for my drinking and mood swings, but I'm not sure how I should begin."

"I've tried to get off drugs cold turkey a few times and failed miserably. I think I could use some professional help."

"I've been abusing my body for far too long. Maybe if I get some treatment, things can be better."

"I've already started cutting back on using, but I need to find some support."

In the preparation stage, you will want to consider *what* you want to change about your life, as well as *how* you plan to make those changes. This is not the place for vague generalities; it's time to get more specific. For instance, if you want to stop smoking, you could choose to enroll in a smoking cessation program, wear a nicotine patch, attend support group meetings, or seek professional help. It's important to make a plan that will fit your lifestyle, but the stronger your choices, the better chance that you will actually follow through with your decision to stop smoking. The same sort of preparation is necessary if you want to stop drinking or doing drugs, lose weight, or quit gambling, hoarding, or engaging in other life-controlling behaviors.

While making these decisions might seem difficult at first, once you get started, you will be pleasantly surprised at how easily you achieve some of your new goals. And of course, with every goal you achieve, your believable hope quotient rises, making it easier to take the next step.

One caution: This plan has to be *yours*, not someone else's. It's okay to draw from other people's experiences in developing their game plans, but to be effective, this plan has to be a meaningful, realistic approach for you.

In developing your plan for transformation, be sure to include these details:

What do I want to change?
What steps will I take to achieve my goals?
What are some possible obstacles I might encounter, and how will
    I overcome them?
Who can help me implement the change I desire?
What are some of my negative thoughts about this change?
What are some of my positive thoughts about making this change?
How will I know the change has been made?

Many people remain in the preparation stage for long periods of time. That's okay. You will only change when *you* are ready, not when someone else coerces you. When you turn around your thinking about change, focusing on where you want to go rather than where you have been, you are ready for the next stage.

Stage Four—Action!

Now we are moving beyond merely thinking and talking about change, or even planning to change; now you are actually taking the steps that will gradually bring about a measurable transformation in your life. A good action plan should include your friends, family, your counselor, mentor, pastor, or sponsor who can help you change your behavior and keep you accountable.

How can you tell when a person is ready to change his or her behavior?

Becoming proactive about the problem is a good sign. You can't just sit back and hope that a negative situation will improve, or a problem or life-controlling issue will simply go away. Like a cavity in a tooth, it will not heal on its own. Action is needed to get rid of the decay and to rebuild the tooth. Something similar is necessary in the mental/emotional areas of life.

In the action stage, you are taking steps every single day—no exceptions—to move toward your goals and modify your behavior. Like many things in life, the first few steps are the most difficult, so don't be too hard on yourself. If you mess up, give yourself plenty of grace, as well as incentives and encouragement to keep trying. Don't get me wrong; I'm not saying that you should take your transformation casually, or that you should be easy on yourself. Transformation takes work. And nobody can do it except you. But I am saying that progress also takes time, and that each small step is a great improvement over where you were. Remember, even baby steps are better than not going forward at all.

The attitude of the person in the action stage sounds like this:

"Every morning I set my goals and do at least one thing that day to help me achieve those goals."

"I admit I have some problems, but I'm committed to getting straightened out."

"I'm following my doctor's advice (or counselor's advice), taking my medicine, praying, and believing for good things in the days ahead."

"I am determined to make a change. If I feel tempted, or slip up in any way, I ask for help. There are people around me who care and are willing to help."

"I know that I can do this. I've seen other people who have been transformed. I now have something I've never had before—believable hope!"

Because you are now committed to changing your mindset, you can much more easily cope with negative thoughts and moods that could undermine your progress. Consider everything by this standard: "Is this activity or attitude helping my transformation or hindering it?" Get in the habit of turning around any negative thoughts and you will soon find that you are feeling better about yourself.

For instance, if you are trying to lose weight, instead of saying, "Oh, no! I've put on three pounds this week! I might as well give up," turn that statement around. "Okay, so I put on three pounds this week. No big deal. I will do better next week. I'll do some research and get some encouragement and suggestions for how I can improve my diet. And I will call my friend Melissa and ask her to walk in the park with me each evening this week after work. I'll knock off those three pounds and more in no time."

As you begin making incremental changes, notice the positive effects these steps are having on you and people around you. You may have more energy, clearer thoughts, and improved memory, or if you are trying to lose weight, you may be able to breathe easier or your cholesterol levels may improve. Whatever good effects you can discover, tout them to yourself, and allow those positive changes to build your confidence. Ask your doctor or therapist what improvements he or she notices. All these things will let you know that you are on the right track. Keep going!

You Don't Have to Go It Alone

While change is usually worth the effort, it is nonetheless hard work. You don't have to be the Lone Ranger, out there doing good on your own (even if you do have Tonto as a sidekick). Although you should accept the ultimate responsibility for your behavior, one of the best things you can do to help you stay committed is to enlist the support of others—your sponsor, therapist, family members, friends, ministers, and support groups such as AA, DRA, NA, and others.

Don't be bashful; plan ahead so you know whom you can call when you need a little motivational oomph. Keep some quick contact information available for several people whom you know will encourage you as you move toward your goals. And don't be reticent to contact them. Circle one or two names in particular that you can contact when you feel desperate or want to give up. Keep several of those names and numbers in your wallet or purse at all times.

Of course, it is equally important to avoid people who might unwittingly sabotage your transformation, or people who are not supportive of the changes you want to make. If you are trying to overcome alcoholism, don't hang out with your former bar buddies, unless they've decided to get sober, too, and have taken similar steps as you have. Remember, talk is cheap. You are now in the action stage. Surround yourself with winners and work your action plan. (We'll get more specific about how to use your action plan in the next section.) Don't surround yourself with people who merely wish to talk about changing. Perhaps they will, but maybe they won't. Avoid any bad influences in your life, and if you can't totally disengage from them, at least try to keep your contact with them to a minimum.

Assuming responsibility for your own transformation may be one of the most profound actions you ever take, and it promises to be one of the most productive as well.

Stage 5—Maintenance

Whether your transformation involves weight issues, drugs or alcohol, sexual addictions, or other compulsive behaviors, when you arrive at the maintenance stage—the level at which you daily perpetuate the good progress you are making—believable hope will help to keep you on track and moving forward.

In the maintenance stage, you are committed to sustaining your changes long-term. It doesn't necessarily mean that you will never again have a problem, or that you won't be tempted, or even that you won't take an occasional step backward. But it does mean that your focus has shifted. You have achieved your initial goals and are working to sustain the positive changes you have made. You are learning to cope with issues in a healthy manner, rather than avoiding them. You now can recognize your triggers and you know how to take steps to keep from succumbing to temptations. (We'll look more closely at maintenance in one of the sections ahead.)

Moreover, since you are now wise to what is going on, you will probably want to keep learning more about how to better cope with your former problems as you continually discover new ways of dealing effectively with situations, people, or other potential triggers. In the maintenance stage, you no longer run away from problems; you learn to handle them. Certainly, there will always be situations you may want to avoid. At other times, you may find it healthier simply to ignore matters that may have formerly bothered you. Regardless, you are free; the negative hold on your life has been broken. You can now live unencumbered by addictions or compulsive behaviors.

That doesn't mean you should stop doing the things that got you to this point. Quite the contrary. If you have been attending a support group such as Alcoholics Anonymous or a similar group, keep showing up at meetings. Not only will you benefit and be encouraged to maintain your progress, but you may also be an inspiration to someone else, just as Pat McDonnell was to me, when I first ventured into an AA meeting.

Living in the maintenance stage allows you to apply the skills you have learned regarding stress management, trigger avoidance, anger management, and other principles you have found that help you to stay clean and make healthy, wise choices. When you feel yourself growing weak, take action to avoid relapses by calling a counselor or a mentor, or someone else who can walk with you through a refresher course in believable hope. Keep your "hope tank" filled, so that you can avoid losing precious ground you have gained.

In the maintenance stage, you are choosing to do the right things the majority of the time. Sure, you may slip up occasionally, but you are quick to get back on track. That's the big difference. It is not that you will never fail, but that when you do make a wrong choice, you correct it as quickly as possible and learn from it.

In the maintenance stage, it is not unusual for you to say things such as

"I like the person I see in my mirror."

"I enjoy making healthy choices regarding my food selections."

"I'm a bit bored and slightly depressed today, so I am going to call a friend and go to a funny movie."

"As long as I continue to work my program and keep to my routine, I'll continue to have more good days than bad."

By the time you reach the maintenance stage, you are convinced that believable hope is not only possible, it is indispensable. You know that you have made positive changes, and your desire is to continue on that path. Keeping your life in balance—counteracting negative situations with positive people and surroundings—is an important aspect of maintaining your progress or helping someone else stay on track.

....

**Believable hope is not only possible,
it is indispensable.**

....

Stage Six—Relapse

The final stage of recovery, as suggested by research psychologists Dr. Carlo DiClemente and Dr. James Prochaska, is understanding, expecting, and dealing with relapse. Since maintaining the life you want involves the anticipation of relapse and is one of my cardinal principles, I won't delve into it further here, except to say that DiClemente and Prochaska are absolutely right. Relapse is a natural and normal part of the rehabilitation process. Relapse can occur at any time and is a part of the recovery process. Anyone who doesn't understand this truth or who naively believes that relapses are indications of failure is setting himself or herself up for major disappointments. Relapses happen. While slipups and backsliding can be discouraging to both someone in rehab as well as family and friends surrounding that person, the experience of relapsing often strengthens a person's resolve to stay clean and sober and to avoid self-destructive habits. You may experience a temporary loss of progress because of a relapse, but if you deal with it promptly and correctly, getting back on track and learning from the experience, you will learn how to better stabilize yourself and continue progressing.

Professional therapists know that the process of change rarely follows a straight, direct path. Often, a person who eventually breaks free of life-controlling issues tends to cycle through the six stages of change several times before he or she achieves a stable life. So don't give up simply because of a relapse.

Certainly, you don't want to condone unhealthy behaviors or attitudes, but two reminders will come in handy. First, don't be surprised when a lapse or relapse occurs. Second, learn to regard a relapse as an opportunity to identify high-risk situations and to choose more effective methods of handling them.

Remember, you are making progress. Even when you feel that you have hit a plateau or that you have had to scramble three steps forward to overcome a setback, you are still far ahead of the place from which you started. Keep looking up and keep moving ahead. Put yourself in a position to succeed and you will!

9

Motivated to Change

If Dr. DiClemente and Dr. Prochaska piqued my imagination about the various stages of change a person must traverse on the way to wholeness, Dr. William R. Miller's work on motivational interviewing totally changed the way I approached helping drug addicts, alcoholics, mentally ill patients, and later, even those who want to lose weight. I became convinced that Dr. Miller's concepts were the best way to help people move through the stages of change.

What Factors Motivate a Person to Change?

Too often, suffering and pain, whether physical or emotional, rudely remind us that we are bruised or broken and we need to find a better way to live. External factors such as a death in the family, a financial setback, or a startling number on a scale can be the jolt that turns on the lightbulb leading to change, but just as frequently, wonderfully positive events in our lives can inspire us to change. When a person gets married, or when you gaze upon your newborn baby for the first time, something within you says, *I want to be better*. Sometimes it can be as simple as sitting on the beach, watching the waves roll in at the end of the day, or the acknowledgment of the grandeur of a gorgeous sunset that puts life in perspective and causes us to want to change.

Age can often be a motivator rather than a reason to be depressed. When John turned fifty, he realized that he was setting himself up for future physical problems if he didn't start taking better care of himself. He deleted sugar and wheat products from his diet and stopped drinking sugar-saturated juices, and he dropped nearly forty pounds before he turned fifty-one. Not only did his cholesterol come down, but his overall energy level went up.

Sometimes taking a new position at work or embarking on a new career can motivate a person to change. When Jerrod Menz and I agreed to bring his residential treatment company, A Better Tomorrow, under the umbrella of American Addiction Centers, Jerrod was eating terribly and was significantly overweight. Before we signed our partnership deal, he and I had an honest conversation in which I confronted him about the issue. "Jerrod, I love ya, buddy, but there is no way we can ignore your weight situation when one of the divisions of our company is a weight-loss program."

Jerrod agreed. "Okay, what can I do?"

"You can come to our treatment center and check in, or I can help you develop a plan." I helped Jerrod develop a game plan for losing weight.

Part of our deal was that he would send me his workout program every day, letting me know exactly what exercises he had done that day. Most days, Jerrod burned more than 800 calories during an hour-long, vigorous workout. He changed his diet and increased his daily intake of water, drinking a half-gallon to a gallon of water every day. Within four months, he had lost forty pounds. By six months, Jerrod had dropped sixty pounds. At this writing, Jerrod has lost more than eighty pounds; he looks great and feels good, too. The new job motivated Jerrod to change, but it was believable hope that helped him do the work necessary to make the change.

Considering all the factors that motivate a person to change, I have found that motivational interviewing is the best way of putting a mirror in front of a person and allowing him or her to see the need for change.

What Is Motivational Interviewing?

Motivational interviewing is not so much a series of techniques, but a way of communicating with and interacting with another person, helping that person to see reality. It is very "other-person" focused, reinforcing change and hopefully providing intrinsic motivation. If a person has only extrinsic factors motivating him or her to change, the desired transformation most likely will not last. On the other hand, by exploring and resolving a person's ambivalence to change, lasting transformation can occur.

Because motivational interviewing is other-person-centered, it is a helpful approach that parents, teachers, coaches, employers, and everyday folks can use. You don't need to be a therapist to practice motivational interviewing. Anyone who is willing can use this method to interact with another human being.

Simply put, rather than attempting to coerce someone to change, or impose change from outside, motivational interviewing is an open conversation between a counselor and a client (or an interventionist and a client, or a family member and a loved one), in which the counselor seeks to strengthen the other person's own motivation and commitment to change. In other words, through the conversation, or a series of conversations, the person sees not only the need for change, but desires to make the necessary change because it is congruent with his or her own values, concerns, and desires. Rather than trying to persuade someone to change against his or her will, a person utilizing Dr. Miller's techniques of motivational interviewing hopes to elicit and explore a person's own reasons for wanting to change.

Not "I'm Right and You're Wrong"

Motivational interviewing, I discovered, has three main elements that are distinctly different from traditional counseling. First, motivational interviewing seeks *collaboration* between the therapist and patient (or the parent and child, or coach and athlete, or teacher and student) rather than *confrontation*. That doesn't mean the therapist or counselor condones the conduct of the patient, or even agrees with the client's assessment of the problem and what should be done. But the counselor does not automatically approach the situation with an "I'm right and you are wrong" attitude. Instead, the counselor seeks to understand where the patient is coming from.

When I was battling my own addictions, most of the therapists who worked with me took a different tack. They came across as the authority or the expert, and most had a "here's looking down on you" attitude, confronting me about my poor choices (I already knew that!), or imposing their perspective on me regarding my substance abuse and mental illness. In most cases, they came up with the plan for my treatment. I'm grateful that the treatment eventually "took," but I can't help wondering if I might have been more open to change had someone worked with me according to Dr. Miller's principles, helping me to embrace change as my own idea, as something I wanted to do, rather than something imposed on me from "above."

Not surprisingly, when I began counseling clients, I quickly fell into a similar pattern of trying to tell a client what was wrong with him or her, and how I thought he or she could best make the necessary changes. Amazingly, some clients really did see that I cared for them, and made the changes in spite of my top-down approach.

When I began using Dr. Miller's ideas of collaboration, however, building rapport and trust with my clients, seeking to understand them, rather than hoping they would understand me, my ability to help people to achieve lasting transformation increased exponentially!

Draw the Person Out

The second key aspect of motivational interviewing that I found refreshing was *evocation*, drawing the other person out, rather than imposing my ideas on him or her. Dr. Miller taught that by drawing out a person's own thoughts and ideas regarding change, rather than imposing the counselor's opinions, the individual is much more likely to make a firm commitment to the necessary actions. When you think about it, that just makes good sense. Most of us prefer to pursue our own ideas rather than being told what to do by someone else. For similar reasons, when an individual decides to change because he or she wants to change, the transformation is much more effective and durable. As such, the therapist's job is to draw out the individual, helping him or her to see the need for change, and the way to achieve it, without telling the person what to do or why they should do it.

The Most Likely Path to Change

The third element of motivational interviewing that fascinated me was the concept of *autonomy* rather than *authority*. Unlike other counseling methods that emphasize the counselor or clinician as the expert or authority figure, motivational interviewing asserts that the real power for lasting change rests with the client. In other words, it is up to the individual to make the change happen. When this is conveyed by word, deed, and attitude by the counselor, the client feels empowered that his or her opinions matter, and that he or she is responsible for the actions that will bring about genuine change. Good counselors tend to reinforce the idea that there is no single, right way to change, and that indeed, there may be a variety of equally enjoyable and effective paths to healthy change. Moreover, the individual is encouraged to take the lead in establishing his or her own game plan that will lead to the desired change.

While this may seem simple, and rather ordinary to some professional clinicians nowadays, when I first began working with clients, this approach was novel. "How can a patient decide what is best for himself or herself?" objecting clinicians protested.

But we soon discovered that Dr. Miller's approach worked. The metaphor Dr. Miller preferred was "dancing" with a client, rather than wrestling with him or her.

How Can You Help Motivate Somebody to Change?

The number one thing anyone can do to help someone else change is to be positive. Support the person in his or her lifestyle change. Understand that you cannot change another person. All you can do is to hold up a mirror to show the person his or her condition. As I learned from Dr. Miller, motivational interviewing is all about how to best approach an addicted person about his or her problem. Professional counselors are helpful, but for years, Alcoholics Anonymous has encouraged individuals who have been clean for long periods of time to become "sponsors," mentors to others who are trying to get clean. Simply knowing someone understands what you are going through and can relate to the problems is often a tremendous help for someone wanting to overcome negative behavior

When you see someone indulging in self-destructive behavior, you can be part of the solution if you engage in realistic and practical interventions. Using these basic motivational interviewing techniques, you can show a person a mirror in which he or she can see himself or herself. Always remember to hug 'em and love 'em. It is far more effective to exude gentleness and kindness, rather than the "in your face" intervention methods that make for good television, but poor results.

When to Seek Professional Help

Understandably, some people do not feel comfortable in trying to help another person get free of drugs or alcohol; they may feel inadequate to intervene with someone addicted to food. Some people are unwilling or feel that they could be easily overwhelmed in such situations. In that case, contact us. We can help you by putting you in contact with highly skilled interventionists in your area who can help you to help the person you care about.

10

Stumbling Blocks to Stepping-Stones

I had been working for the co-op for more than two years when I began to mull over a recurring idea. It was a dream that simply would not go away. The more I thought about it, the more convinced I became that I wanted to start a halfway house for men who were dealing with both alcoholism or drug addiction and some form of psychosis or other mental illnesses. Most rehabilitation programs at the time leaned one way or the other, either toward the Alcoholics Anonymous approach of using no substitutes to help beat the compulsive behavior, or the opposite, which was espoused by most mental health professionals to medicate the person dealing with addictive or compulsive behavior. I wanted to pull from both sides of the spectrum and help people get free one way or the other, or both.

Tina and I were not yet married at that time, but she saw the need, too. She had worked with enough addicts and alcoholics to know that there was a piece missing from the treatment puzzle. At our best, we were doing only half the job by not addressing the mental illness that afflicts so many people with compulsive behaviors. Tina believed in my dream for a halfway house, but like me, she wasn't making a lot of money. We were frustrated because we saw a tremendous need, but didn't have the resources to do anything about it.

One day I was listening to a popular, nationally syndicated radio talk show, hosted by Dave Ramsey and broadcast live from Nashville. I was a big fan of Dave's, mainly because his financial advice sounded a lot like my grandmother's. I decided to call the show and get Dave's opinion on my idea of creating a halfway house for drug addicts and alcoholics. I dialed the number and told the call screener about my question.

"Stay on the line," she said. "You'll be on the air with Dave in just a few minutes." She instructed me to formulate my question in the most concise manner while I waited and listened to the show through the phone.

When Dave came on, I quickly outlined my plan to him, explaining briefly how I wanted to help people with mental illness and substance abuse, on both ends of the addiction and mental health spectrum, by opening a halfway house where both could be treated.

Dave loved the idea. Until, that is, he began quizzing me about my own financial status. "How much do you make a year?" he asked.

"Sixteen thousand dollars," I told him.

"Sixteen grand?" Dave echoed, the surprise evident in his voice. "And how much do you have in savings?"

"Well, I don't really have anything in savings right now."

"And do you have your $1,000 emergency fund in place?" Dave pressed. "What are you going to do if your car breaks down? Do you have any money laid aside for those kinds of everyday emergencies?"

"No, not really."

"Let me get this straight. You don't have any money in savings; you earn 16K a year, and you don't have an emergency fund, and yet you want to open a halfway house for drug addicts and alcoholics—who probably aren't going to be able to pay you a lot. . . ." Dave's voice was building in intensity. "Do I have that right?"

"Yes, that's what I want to do. And I'd like to develop a dual-diagnosis treatment center, and start a business out of that. What do you think?"

"You can't!" Dave almost yelled into his studio microphone. "You shouldn't and you can't!" Dave went on to slam my idea into the ground. It wasn't so much the idea that he opposed; he just thought the idea of me doing it was ridiculous. "You're broke!" he said. "Stay at your job, save some money, and when you can open your business by paying cash, then fine. Do whatever you want. But until then, forget it!"

I was shattered. The guy on the radio, whose financial advice I highly respected, had poured cold water all over the sparks of my dream.

Later that evening, I stopped by to visit my grandmother. I told her, "Grandma, you're not going to believe this, but I called Dave Ramsey on the radio and told him about my idea, that I want to help mentally ill drug addicts and alcoholics by opening a halfway house for men who have psychosis and substance abuse issues. . . ."

"What?" Grandmother interrupted me. "Why would you do that? Are you crazy? They'll burn down your house!"

Now I was really discouraged. My favorite radio talk show host and my favorite person in the whole wide world had both told me the same thing, that starting a halfway house for mentally ill men and substance abusers was a bad idea.

But I was convinced otherwise. Why? Because I had been there. I had been in the mental hospitals; I had spent five months in a psych ward, and I had also gone through the Alcoholics Anonymous program, and I knew that nobody was adequately treating both sides of the spectrum. I was convinced that most individuals dealing with compulsive issues desperately needed a dual-diagnosis program, where both the addiction and the illness could be addressed.

Over the next few months, I kept coming back to Grandma Cartwright again and again, explaining my dream to her. I didn't have the financial resources to open the halfway house, nor did my parents. But Grandma had some resources. She owned more than twenty rental properties in Nashville, as well as several apartment complexes. So every chance I got, I pressed her, "Grandma, I want to open a halfway house and I was hoping you would let me use one of your rental properties."

"What? You need to get a better job and finance your own house. How much money do you make, anyhow?"

"My job pays around $16,000 a year."

"You're not going to be able to support your wonderful girlfriend on that kind of salary."

"What have you always told me?" I asked. "What did you tell me I should do with my life? You said, 'Do what you love; forget about the money, and do what you are passionate about, and you will enjoy life. Because money doesn't make you happy. It's being passionate about what you do that really brings satisfaction.' Grandma, I love helping people; I especially love helping people with mental illness; I love helping them get off drugs and alcohol and other addictions. I love seeing them get better."

· ·

Do what you love; forget about the money,
and do what you are passionate about,
and you will enjoy life.

· ·

I could see Grandma's demeanor softening. "Yes, you are right," she said quietly. Little by little, she began to lean more in my direction. Because of her belief in me, I felt sure that Grandma would buy into my idea and help me finance the halfway house. But she wouldn't budge.

After about six months of my badgering, trying to persuade her of the need for and the viability of the halfway house, Grandmother was getting closer. But it wasn't my logic or powers of persuasion that softened her. One of the main reasons she accepted the idea was my girlfriend, Tina. Grandma loved Tina, and if Tina believed in the halfway house idea, Grandma could live with it.

On Tuesday evening before Thanksgiving, Grandma finally succumbed to our pressure. "Okay, I'll help you out," Grandma said. "There's a house up for auction this Saturday and it might work for your purposes, so we'll go take a look at it. If it is a good property, I'll buy it and you can live in it when you get married, or you can use it for your halfway house."

I was so excited. Finally, Grandmother was going to help us get our business off the ground. Grandmother invited Tina and me to her home on Thursday for Thanksgiving dinner, but Tina was working at the city mission that day, dishing up Thanksgiving dinner for homeless folks. We'd all get together on Saturday and we would go see the house. My dream was about to come true.

I arrived at Grandma Cartwright's house around ten o'clock in the morning on Thanksgiving Day. Ordinarily, Grandma always put the turkey in the oven early in the morning to allow it to cook ever so slowly, so as soon as I stepped through the front door, I expected the aroma of perfectly seasoned turkey to greet me. But the house was oddly devoid of the mouthwatering scents.

I peeked in the dining room and saw that the table was not yet impeccably set with Grandma's best china and crystal. That struck me as unusual, too. "Grandma," I called. "I'm here. It's Michael."

No answer.

I figured that she might be in the bathroom, so I went on inside the house and made myself comfortable. A few more minutes passed and still Grandma had not shown her face.

"Grandma," I called out again, "are you okay? It's Michael. Can I help you in any way?"

Still no answer.

"Something's not right," I said aloud to myself, stepping back inside. "Grandma, where are you?" I yelled. I was getting concerned now. I went to the back of the house where Grandma's bedroom was located. The door was shut. "Grandma, are you in there? It's Michael. Are you okay?"

Silence.

"Grandma, don't be afraid; it's me, Michael, and I'm coming in." I slowly pushed the door open and immediately spied Grandma, still in bed, the covers pulled up around her shoulders.

"Grandma?" I hurried across the room and gently shook my grandmother's arm. "Grandma? Are you sleeping? Don't you feel well?"

She didn't respond.

"Grandma!"

I checked Grandma Cartwright's breathing, her heart and pulse, tears already trickling down my face.

About that time, my uncle came upstairs from where he had been working down in the basement. He called 911, but the coldness of Grandma's skin told us that she must have slipped away in the night.

I was devastated. Grandma Cartwright was my best friend in the world. Tina, of course, was well on her way to dislodging Grandma from the number-one spot in my heart, but at the time, Grandma still owned it. She was the premier influence in my life. Now she was gone.

Ironically, a mere three months earlier, Grandma Cartwright had called me into her bedroom one day and said, "Michael, I want you to know where my lockbox is, and my insurance policies. Here's where I want to be buried, and by the way, I just want you to know that I have taken you out of my will."

"What?" I was shocked. "Why would you do that? Have I done something wrong? I'm clean and sober. Have I offended you in some way?" It didn't make any sense.

"No," Grandma said with a smile, "nothing like that. You are doing so well, and I don't want to demotivate you in life. I don't want to enable you. If I leave you a bunch of money, houses, or property in my will, you won't struggle for it. You won't enjoy the privilege of making it on your own. It's so much more fun when you make it on your own."

"Grandma?" I heard what she was saying, but the logic of it escaped me. It would take me a number of years to learn the truth of Grandma's statement and even more time to appreciate the wisdom of it. What I considered a stumbling block, Grandma knew could be a stepping-stone.

Now, however, I had to notify our relatives and let them know that Grandma had passed away.

Her funeral was well attended since my grandparents had become prominent in the Nashville business community. Then at the reading of Grandmother's will, the secret that I already knew was revealed to other members of the family.

"I'm sorry to tell you that your grandmother removed you from her final will and testament," my uncle told me.

"Yes, I know," I said. "And here's where you can find the keys to her strong box, and here's a list of her bank accounts." I handed over the documents.

True to her word, Grandma left me nothing in her will. She did, however, leave a large amount of property to my dad, so all hope for assistance with the halfway house was not lost.

Not until I asked him. "Dad, you may not be aware of this, but a few days before she died, Grandma promised me that she would help me get a house where I could start a halfway house for drug addicts, alcoholics, and mentally ill men."

"Really?" Dad said with a nod. "She said that, did she?"

"Yes, she did. So I was wondering if maybe you could let me use one of the houses that she left to you in her will, and allow me to turn it into a halfway house to help men with substance abuse and mental health issues?"

Dad stroked his chin as though he were thinking over the matter. But as soon as he spoke, I could tell that he wasn't interested. "Well, no, son, I don't think I can afford to do that right now. I need the income."

"Dad, Grandma left you a bunch of money and a bunch of houses. I just need one small house to get started."

"No, sorry, I really can't do that," Dad said. "But good luck with your idea. I hope that comes together for you."

I had no money and very little good credit, so I decided I would have to raise the money for the halfway house. I enrolled in a class on entrepreneurship at Tennessee State University and wrote a ten-page business plan on the concept of dual diagnosis, the need for combining treatment for mental illness and addictive behaviors, building a halfway house, renting it to men, and running it as a business.

As soon as I completed the class, I approached almost every friend I knew who had any money and asked them if they wanted to invest in my idea. None did.

I presented my business plan to anyone who might have some money and was willing to read it. The plan didn't evoke a lot of excitement, especially since I intended to help inner-city, homeless men with schizophrenia and addictions—drug addicts, alcoholics, and mentally ill men, most of whom were unable to pay for the services I hoped to offer. It felt as though my dream was slipping away again, but I refused to give up.

Grandma had always encouraged me to surround myself with good people, so I set out on a quest to find some new friends.

11

A Light in the Darkness

One of the first things they tell you in Alcoholics Anonymous is to get away from all your playmates and playthings from the past. Why? If you go back to your former environment, hanging out with your former friends who are most likely still doing the things you were doing, you can easily relapse. In fact, almost inevitably, if you don't make a clean break with those negative influences, you *will* relapse.

Instead, surround yourself with winners, with the world you want to create, with people who don't drink or do drugs. If you want to lose weight, spend most of your time with people who don't overeat or regularly indulge in destructive behaviors. If you want to get free from addictive behaviors, you must think differently and act differently. Go to meetings where other people are fighting similar battles as you.

Find a sponsor, a mentor, someone who will share insights with you and be a role model for you, and hopefully help keep you accountable by encouraging you to stay on the right track. Choose your mentors wisely, though. As best-selling author Rick Warren advises, "Never ask anyone to be your mentor until first you know who his or her mentors have been and currently are."[10]

Before I started my own behavioral health-care company, I read everything I could find about how great companies operate, not simply their production plans, but more importantly, their attitudes and approaches toward business. I attended business and motivational seminars; I did all that I could to change my perspective and any ingrained negative ways of thinking.

I sought out business mentors, fifty- or sixty-year-old guys who were thriving entrepreneurs. A key mentor in my life was Bob Nash, a highly successful businessman in Nashville, who I actually met before I conquered my own compulsive behaviors.

As a young man, barely out of my teens, I was strung out on drugs and alcohol and obsessed with finding some way to make money. I attended a celebration party for Dick Clark (no, not *that* Dick Clark), a local legislator who had just been elected to office from the district in which my parents lived. There was an open bar at the party and I was making a rather obvious fool of myself by drinking too much and on the verge of acting inappropriately when a friend of mine pointed out Bob Nash to me. "See that guy over there. You need to get to know him. He's the kind of guy you want to connect with."

I boldly approached Mr. Nash and introduced myself. "Mr. Nash, I'm Michael Cartwright, and I am honored to meet you."

Nash was kind, cordial, and polite but he could probably tell that I was teetering precariously on the precipice of inebriation, so he quickly moved on to the next person waiting to greet him.

Undeterred, the following week, I called Bob Nash. "Mr. Nash, this is Michael Cartwright, and I met you at the Dick Clark party last week. I'd love to take you to lunch sometime this week."

Nash was noncommittal. "Thank you, Michael, but I don't have time. My schedule is rather full this week. Call me back some other time."

Call me back?

"Okay, I will." And I did. Every week for the next four months, I called Bob Nash and invited him to lunch with me. Every time I called, he politely declined my invitation. "Mr. Nash, this is Michael Cartwright, following up with you about lunch."

"Sorry, son. I don't have time."

"Well, how about next week?"

"No, sorry; I'm already committed next week, too."

We went through this same routine for four straight months. I refused to give up. It's a miracle he still accepted my phone calls!

But he did. And then one day when I called, his response changed. "Okay, Michael, let's go to lunch today."

Today? You betcha! I'll be right there.

At lunch, I reintroduced myself to Bob Nash—he hadn't seen me in four months, and then only briefly when I was nearly sloshed—and I told him, "Mr. Nash, I want to be an entrepreneur and I want to learn from a man like you. How can I do that?"

"Watch what I do, and do something similar," he responded.

That's all I needed to hear. I practically attached myself to Bob Nash. Wherever he went, I went, insofar as he would permit. I asked him a million questions and took note of every answer. He was always kind and gracious and didn't seem to mind my oftentimes naïve questions.

He actually seemed to enjoy sharing about his business principles and the steps he had taken—both positively and negatively—that helped lead him to the successful lifestyle he now enjoyed. In the process, we became inseparable friends. We did everything together, went to parties and sporting events together, drank far too much together, and did drugs together.

Not surprisingly, when Bob decided that he wanted to get clean and sober, I followed his example. Actually I had little choice if I wanted to maintain our friendship. "I can't be around you," Bob told me straightforwardly, "unless you stop drinking." So I did. Clearly, the power of a mentor in your life can be tremendously transformational and enormously beneficial.

> **The power of a mentor can
> be tremendously transformational.**

Bob Nash made the transformation physically, spiritually, and financially as he left drugs and alcohol behind. In the process, he read every book and listened to every tape series he could find on positive thought. It took him a number of years to make the complete transformation from living with addictions in abject poverty to becoming a multimillionaire, living with health and freedom from drugs and alcohol. But he did it. I wanted to learn from a man like that.

The Power of a Positive Partner

Naturally, when I began looking for investors for the halfway house, Bob's name instantly came to mind. Bob listened attentively as I made my pitch. I began by explaining to him the need for a treatment center that brought together the two main approaches to dealing with alcoholism and drug addictions on the one hand, and mental illnesses on the other.

"Bob, you know that Alcoholics Anonymous, for example, wants a person to get clean with no artificial help, no ongoing mind-altering drugs or medications. On the other hand, most people in the mental illness field feel that the only way many mental issues can be helped is by keeping the person on medication, sometimes for life. But there's a real need for someone to treat people who are in the center, that have both: addiction issues as well as mental illnesses. I'm not saying it has to be an either-or situation. I'm convinced that many people are like me, who needed to be classified with a dual diagnosis, with both mental illness and addiction issues. I want to do something to help that group of people in the middle who are suffering both problems."

Although dual diagnosis was a relatively new concept, Bob could easily understand the need within the addiction field to treat people with co-occurring disorders. Earlier in his life, he had won his own battles against addiction, so he could relate. I could tell this was going to be a mission of passion for him more than a mere speculative, moneymaking venture.

One day, not long after Grandma Cartwright had passed away, I called Bob and said, "I want you to see something."

I had found a house in East Nashville on McKinney Avenue, and I envisioned it as the halfway house we could develop. The house was huge, with ten or twelve rooms. The husband and wife who owned it were going through a divorce and simply wanted out of it. They were willing to negotiate on the price.

Bob agreed to meet me in East Nashville to check out the house as one he might be interested in purchasing for us to use as the halfway house. I was looking at the house as a place for treating alcoholics, addicts, and mentally ill men, but Bob was looking at the house as a potential financial investment. He showed up wearing his best real estate hat, examining everything about the property.

What Bob didn't know was that I had borrowed $500 from Tina by taking a $500 cash advance on her credit card, and I had already made a deposit on the home as earnest money. If Bob didn't like the place, not only was I going to be out $500, I was going to be out $500 of my girlfriend's money! I was sweating bullets as Bob went through each room of the house, stomping on the floor, listening for squeaks in the floorboards, tapping on pipes, looking for leaks in the ceilings, flushing the toilets, and trying to determine if it was really worth the money the couple was asking.

What Bob didn't tell me was that the moment he pulled up in front of the house and realized the size, location, and price, he determined right then and there that he was going to buy the house! But he didn't tell me that as he went through his meticulous inspection.

At the end of the day, Bob said, "Okay, Michael, I'll buy the house, and we'll become partners. You can use it for the halfway house and when we sell it, we'll split half of the profits."

I couldn't agree soon enough.

The Right Kind of Partner

The first halfway house we opened in East Nashville had room for eight male residents. From 1995 to 1997 we had only one house in which we provided all services to the residents. The money the men paid (mostly by means of their disability checks) barely covered the expenses of housing, feeding, and caring for them. Our first year, we took in $60,000 and spent $80,000. The second year we fared little better, with our income reaching $120,000, while our expenses exceeded $140,000. Tina and I did everything from scrubbing the floors to feeding and counseling the men. We did it all. We weren't making any money, but the halfway house was a passion project for Tina and me. We loved helping people, especially those we recognized who needed our dual-diagnosis approach. In a real sense, it was basically a charity project funded by my partner, Bob Nash, and directed for free by me. Fortunately, Bob had enough confidence in me that he allowed me time to figure out how to monetize our services.

In the rehab world, a counselor usually doesn't have to wait long before the case load fills up. One of my early clients at the halfway house made a profound impression on me. When I first met Glen, he was a homeless paranoid schizophrenic living on the streets of Nashville. He looked literally like something the cat might have dragged into the house—dirty, disheveled, unkempt. He was one of the most chronic mentally ill individuals I've ever worked with. Our first order of business was to help him feel better about himself, and that involved getting clean. Amazing what a hot shower and shave can do for a person.

Of course, Glen's challenges were much more than skin deep. He had profound issues that had caused him to be separated from his wife and barred from seeing his eleven-year-old daughter. But when he came through our doors, he was seeking help and ready to change.

I began working with him in individual sessions, as well as in group therapy. I was Glen's lifeline to reality, and he held on tightly. Change didn't come quickly or easily. I stayed in the trenches with him for nearly four years, but Glen emerged as a new person, a healthy, productive member of society. His crowning achievement, of course, was the day he was reunited with his daughter. I was nearly overwhelmed with emotion as I watched a "new" father embrace his daughter. Glen's story of transformation was so amazing that he was awarded the prestigious Ely Lilly Award, alongside the Mental Health Commissioner of Missouri and researchers from the National Institutes of Health.

About two years later, Bob, Tina, and I met about another deal. I had found a location on Division Street, near Nashville's famous Music Row, where I wanted to open an outpatient treatment center. Bob liked the idea, and even suggested that we bring in Dick Clark as our attorney.

Bob looked across the table at Tina and me and spoke straight-forwardly. "If we do this today, I am 95 percent of the business and you are 5 percent. Your contribution to the business is very small; my contribution is huge. But there will come a day when you will be 95 percent of the business, and I will be 5 percent. And that will be okay with me."

I appreciated Bob's wisdom and his confidence in Tina and me. I smiled back at him appreciatively, grateful for his willingness to partner with us, but in truth, we were dependent on Bob.

> He who walks with the wise grows wise, but a companion of fools suffers harm.
>
> —*Proverbs 13:20 (New International Version)*

While others may have questioned my transformation early on, Bob Nash never doubted that I had changed, that I was free of drugs and alcohol. He wasn't worried that I would relapse and slip back into my former lifestyle. He recognized that I was ready to help others with substance issues, and although he was a businessman and not a therapist, Bob believed that I had some answers worth sharing with others.

Some Skeptics Never Believe

A number of my former friends, however, could hardly believe that I was free of drugs and alcohol. Even my father was skeptical. He was so accustomed to me using drugs and alcohol, it took me two years to convince him that I was clean, and even then he credited Tina for helping me to get sober. I didn't actually meet Tina until two years after I'd gotten clean and sober, but my father was still convinced that Tina changed my life. She did, but not quite as soon as Dad thought!

Although Dad's timing was off, his point is worth considering. Having the right partner in life is critical to any success. Had Tina been a drug user or an alcohol abuser, no matter how hard I tried to stay clean, it probably would have been impossible on a long-term basis. Fortunately for me, Tina did not do drugs or alcohol; quite the opposite. When we met, she and I worked together at Mental Health Cooperative, and then later at the halfway house, helping men and women get free from their addictions.

> **Having the right partner in life is**
> **critical to any success.**

The halfway house was set up originally as a nonprofit organization, so for the first four years, I worked without a salary. But in the year 2000, Tina's and my first child, our son Alexander, was born. Suddenly the responsibility of being a husband and a father hit me with full force, as I began thinking about how I was going to make a living for my family.

We had lived on Tina's salary during those four years while I was building our business. She believed in my dream that we could do something so good that it would eventually pay off, so she worked constantly to keep us above water. I appreciated her willingness to sacrifice many of the normal amenities of life, much less the luxuries of life, so we could serve hurting people. But with children in the mix, I became much more intentional about making our business a financial success as well as a benefit to our community.

The third year of our operation, I convinced Bob to invest more money, and we opened our first outpatient clinic in 1997. We began the facility initially as a not-for-profit venture, though we later discovered that wasn't the smartest idea. Nevertheless, we all pitched in to do whatever was necessary to get the building in shape. We called the outpatient facility Foundations Associates, a place where people could establish new foundations in their lives. Bob financed the entire operation, and I ran it.

Do What You Love and . . .

Bob was a bottom-line sort of guy. After struggling to get the doors open, Bob was anxious to see the treatment facility full. It was touch and go for quite a while. "Fellows, we're in trouble," he told us bluntly one day. "We have rent and other obligations coming due soon. We're going to need to pay some bills, and we have no money coming in. I want some butts in seats!"

Imagine how thrilled Bob was when he stopped by the clinic a few weeks later and saw all the counseling rooms as well as the waiting room filled with people. "Wow, how many people do we have in there?" Bob asked with a big smile, certain that his motivational speech had stimulated our growth in the number of clients.

"Twenty," I told him.

"That's incredible! How much money do we make from that?"

"Money? These clients aren't paying anything. We don't make any profit," I admitted rather sheepishly. "We don't have an insurance contract yet, so we don't really get paid. We've been treating people for free."

"For free? What in the world kind of business is this? How can you do that?"

In truth, none of us were making any money; that's how we could do it. That was the only way. I pulled into work each morning in a beat-up, $900 pickup truck, spewing enough smoke from its exhaust pipe that it's a wonder I didn't get arrested for polluting the air!

Fortunately, we had a lot of volunteers who helped make the facility function; otherwise we would have had to close the doors. Some key lawyers, counselors, and other professional people came to our aid, offering their services for free, as did many volunteers from area churches, and together we did whatever we had to do to help provide a safe, caring environment for the addicts and alcoholics we were trying to help. It was truly a labor of love. But as even the most idealistic romanticist will admit, it's hard to live on love.

After working night and day for more than four years, I came home from work one night totally discouraged. We had started with such lofty dreams for Foundations Associates, but it just wasn't working. We were still trying to get our nonprofit status so we could work with Medicaid patients, which would provide a regular source of funding, but for some reason, everything was taking longer than expected. Bob told me bluntly, "Michael, I don't want to put any more money into this if we are not going to be able to turn it around." Tina had gone back to work with a managed-care company, and she and I were dumping gobs of our own money into the business, and weren't receiving anything in return.

When I came home down and depressed, Tina quickly picked up on my mood. "What's the matter?" she asked.

"I just don't think we can make it," I answered sullenly. "We've been at this for four years, and we haven't made a penny. We can't get the Medicaid contracts, and you and I are pouring money into this business. Maybe I should just close it up, and go get a job so I can work to pay back Bob over time."

If I was expecting sympathy from Tina, I was fooling myself. "What?" Tina retorted. "Are you kidding me? I have never heard you talking like this. You're always positive. This is not you, and you don't need to be acting like this. Snap out of it! You just better figure it out."

Tina's straightforward rebuke was like getting hit in the face by a bucket full of cold water; it snapped me out of despair and brought me quickly to my senses. No more feeling sorry for myself. I went back to work with a fresh passion and an intense focus on figuring out how our treatment center could move from nonprofit to a productive, profit-making business.

The obvious answer was to create a for-profit side to our facility and treatment center that could still provide services to indigents and others who could not afford to pay for the services, but we could be paid by the state or local community for providing the services. Within six months, the state finally came through with a grant, and we picked up some federal contracts as well. We hired our first staff member, Janna Aiken, who has continued working with me to this day.

At the time, I knew very little about running a business, but Grandmother Cartwright had taught me, "Surround yourself with good people, people who know more than you do, or have skills that you don't have." That's what I did; I surrounded myself with good people, careful to pick the right people for the right job, and that made all the difference. If I made a mistake in selecting an employee, I was quick to recognize that and rectified the situation as soon as possible. I was also determined to pay our employees well. They were serving desperate, hurting people from their hearts; the last thing I wanted them to worry about was their own subsistence.

··

Surround yourself with
good people.

··

We also got some breaks by drawing the right people in state offices to assist us. For example, Melanie Hampton, the director of the Tennessee Mental Health Department, helped tremendously in getting funding, including an initial grant from the state of Tennessee for $500,000, as well as Medicaid contracts with the government. The director's expertise was a lifesaver for all of us.

I learned as we went. It took nearly five years before we became a profitable business. From 1995 to 1999, we inched along like we had concrete blocks on our feet. But from 1999 to 2004, we grew exponentially. By then, we were a full-fledged rehabilitation facility, complete with psychiatrists working for us, an aftercare program, and a fully functional pharmacy to help serve our clients. We even helped clients find employment after going through our program. We were still serving the indigent population, but at least we now had access to funding from Medicare and Medicaid, as well as state contracts. Bob eventually sold his portion of the company to me in July 2005, but we remained close friends. I knew we'd be in business together again before long.

A New Way of Looking at
Life-Controlling Issues

In the process of building our treatment centers, I became active in championing dual diagnosis. At that time, addictions and mental illnesses were rarely treated concurrently, but usually considered as separate issues. I was convinced that more often than not, self-destructive, compulsive behaviors and mental or emotional problems fed upon each other. Indeed, in my research, I found that nearly 70 percent of the people with drug or alcohol addictions had a co-occurring mental or emotional problem as well. Yet most people were never treated for both issues simultaneously.

Since I had studied dual diagnosis so thoroughly, and had dealt directly with so many patients, I became known as an expert on the subject. As part of my work on the topic, over a seven-year period, our company conducted fifteen independent, federally funded research studies on dual diagnosis, including studies on adolescents as well as adults. At first we drew researchers from Vanderbilt University, and eventually we created our own research institute.

Senator Edward "Ted" Kennedy's office invited me to participate on a committee concerning substance abuse. Besides it being a tremendous honor and a learning experience for me, I felt that we were truly on the cusp of new approaches to treating addictions, and the Senate-sponsored committee incorporated dual diagnosis into our recommendations, all of which were seriously considered, and many of which were implemented.

Out of that grew the President's Task Force on Co-Occurring Disorders, a group of doctors, mental health workers, advocates, researchers, and other experts who studied the issues and made recommendations to the president. As a result, treatment centers—especially those receiving government funds—made tangible changes in helping people with co-occurring disorders. Since 2002, through our advocacy, many more improvements in dealing with dual diagnosis have been made, and that gives me a tremendous sense of gratification. Now, we were not only helping people in Nashville, but from our humble, meager efforts, Tina, Bob, and I were providing information and help to people all across the United States and to various parts of the world.

While pushing forward the need for dual diagnosis, I met Tim Hamilton, a young man who had formed a Dual Recovery Anonymous group, using a twelve-step program similar to the renowned Alcoholics Anonymous approach to help people with addictions in combination with mental/emotional issues. At the time, this approach was rare in the rehabilitation field, much less in the support field. I recognized immediately the value of what Tim was doing, and over the next five years, I helped him promote the concept of DRA and set up chapters internationally. I convinced Tim to move to Nashville so we could work together more closely, and I funded Dual Recovery Anonymous, the informational packets, as well as a new website for the organization.

Tim and I traveled together from coast to coast, and everywhere we went, we talked constantly of how we had discovered believable hope. Today, someone seeking help can find a Dual Recovery Anonymous group in most cities in the United States, and most major locations around the world. To date, the DRA meetings have helped hundreds of thousands of people, and the numbers continue to climb.

Eventually our business outgrew our office space on Division Street in Nashville, so I talked with Bob about buying a building. Bob thought it might be wiser to lease office space, but I preferred to own it—with the help of Bob's money, of course. Within a week or two, I found an office building in Nashville's Metro Center. Bob and I worked out the same sort of arrangement as the deal we had previously: Bob would buy the building and remodel it, and I would run our operations from it. I provided the team and the talent, and Bob provided the physical plant. Then if we decided to sell, we'd split the profits.

Before long, I had another idea for Bob to consider. I wanted to build a series of apartments for low-income individuals who completed our rehabilitation and aftercare programs. No matter how much of a transformation they made while under our care, they would need a decent place to live once they were on their own, a safe place where they could call home. I explained my vision to Bob: I could see a person on the street, drug addicted or psychotic, and then I could picture that same person conquering his or her addictions. I could see that person in a stable home, with a job, and perhaps even starting a family. I wanted to provide whatever was needed all along the way, to get that person from point A to point B, from addiction to freedom. Bob listened carefully to my ideas, and then we'd go to work trying to find a way to make them happen.

Bob wasn't surprised when I came in one day and told him that I had found a facility for sale in Memphis that had formerly been owned by a hospital, a nonprofit organization, so by law, they had to sell it to another nonprofit. Foundations qualified. Bob and I traveled to Memphis to check out the possibilities. The property needed a great deal of work, but we could see tremendous potential. We bought the old hospital and refurbished it to house residential rehabilitation clients.

We already had ten residential facilities in Nashville, but we went ahead and opened a 120-bed facility in Memphis, too.

Our business was growing rapidly, so we continually looked for ways to better finance it. A fantastic boon came our way when the company for which Tina worked agreed to give us a contract to audit medical files in the Atlanta area. We created a new company known as Dual Diagnosis Management (DDM). Our job was to audit every state-funded mental health center in Georgia, getting their client information in top-notch shape, so when the files were presented to the federal government for payment, there would be no question about the validity of the treatment or the expenses. Tina knew that business well, so she helped set up our auditing program and we hired incredibly talented people. We hired her former boss and her boss's boss, and within twelve months, we had contracts in four states. From there, our business took off.

The day-to-day business was originally focused on assessment contracts, to determine the level of care needed for people with mental retardation. Then we branched out and began doing the research contracts. The best part about our success with Dual Diagnosis Management was that it gave us the financial resources to operate the treatment centers populated by people who couldn't afford to pay, or for whom the government was willing to pay very little. But there was still a huge hole in our system, a tremendous need that we were missing.

12

Movin' On Up

One day I walked into the office and told Bob, "We need to do something to separate our homeless clients from our professional, executive clients." At the time, we had professional types staying in the same locations as homeless people. I recognized that although the protocol may be the same, and the treatments may be similar, the clients simply couldn't relate to each other. A wealthy, executive type of client simply felt uncomfortable around clients who had come off the streets, and vice versa: the homeless clients felt intimidated or awkward around the businesspeople, and sometimes even a bit hostile toward a more affluent client. It was an untenable situation, so we began looking for a place where we could better treat executive-style clients.

I was still working in our local halfway house in Nashville; I enjoyed my work serving in the inner city, and had no illusions of ever getting rich from it. During the winter of 2003, however, I met a man who would expand my horizons and change my perspective forever. His name was Fred Segal.

Fred was already a highly successful, California-based food and clothing business entrepreneur who had influenced the world by making designer jeans acceptable and cool to wear, opening the door especially for women to don attractive—and expensive—designer jeans. In 1960, Fred created the first jeans-only story in Santa Monica. His signature "Fred Segal" stores have been immortalized in numerous movies and several pop songs.

In addition to his food and clothing businesses, Segal owned a jewelry business, beauty salons, cafés, and a struggling drug and alcohol treatment facility in Malibu that Fred wanted to turn into a high-end, executive-type rehabilitation center known as the Canyon.

I met Fred through Lee McCormick, who ran a rehabilitation center in East Tennessee and was already acquainted with Fred. I had proven myself to Lee McCormick, because I had been successful in the public sector, setting up facilities and turning around hospitals and other agencies, making them profitable. Lee told Fred, "Michael Cartwright is the guy who can make this program work. We need to get him involved. There are a lot of people doing rehabilitation programs around the country, but Michael is the best when it comes to both the clinical side as well as the business. There are plenty of mom-and-pop operations out there, but they don't know all facets of the rehabilitation industry and how to scale it upward, to handle a high-end clientele. Others can handle the job once it is going, but few can develop what we need as a start-up operation. Michael can help us do that."

I traveled to California to check out the center. At the time, the Malibu facility was not doing well. But it was on a picturesque 300-acre property and had great potential. Fred invited me to stay in California as a consultant, to help set up the facilities and the programs at the Canyon. I did everything from hiring doctors to deciding what colors the walls should be painted to create a warm, peaceful environment, one that would be conducive to rehabilitation. Before long, I wanted to purchase the business from Fred. Segal said, "Make me an offer."

A few months later, we opened our first high-end, private drug and alcohol rehabilitation center in Malibu, California. Our partner in the venture, Fred Segal, leased the property to us. Before long, we purchased the place outright. By implementing a program with top-notch medical personnel combined with good business practices, the facility was soon full. Because of the beautiful location and the type of clients we treated there, the Malibu center soon became well known. Clients seeking confidential therapy came from all across the nation. We helped a number of high-profile, celebrity-type individuals who would be recognizable on television or in movies today.

With the Canyon's success, we gave our facility in Memphis another makeover, to make it more attractive to professionals and executive-type clients, and solidified our position as one of the best resources in the world where people could turn to find help for alcoholism and drug addiction.

Today, as the chairman of the board of American Addiction Centers, I help oversee the operations of an ever-widening array of transformational services and facilities. One of our recent acquisitions was the Greenhouse, formerly known as the Greenhouse Spa in the Dallas area. Built originally in 1965 by Stanley Marcus, founder of the Neiman Marcus department store chain, the Greenhouse is a nationally recognized luxury spa that historically has been a destination retreat for such high-profile celebrities as Grace Kelly, Cindy Crawford, Lady Bird Johnson, and Barbara Bush. Since purchasing and updating the property, we now use the Greenhouse as a drug and alcohol treatment center for clients who prefer high-end accommodations and attention.

American Addiction Centers has also partnered with A Better Tomorrow, a residential treatment center, as well as intensive outpatient programs in various locations throughout Southern California. We also have a beautiful treatment center in Las Vegas, known as Desert Hope.

As part of our emphasis on living a healthy life, we opened Fit-RX, a weight-loss retreat center near Nashville. Fit-RX provides people with the tools, training, education, and support they need to lose weight, look good, feel better, and live longer by establishing long-term, practical, workable solutions to food addiction. We help individuals transform their own lives by teaching them not only what to eat but how to prepare the food. I realized how difficult it was to lose weight and keep it off when I was challenged to drop more than seventy pounds. It took work, but I did it.

None of these positive changes in my life would have happened had I not learned, as Grandma said, to surround myself with good people. The same will be true for you. If you want to experience a lasting transformation, stay in a positive environment as much as possible. Avoid negative, compromising situations or people who consciously or unwittingly sabotage your efforts, and instead, surround yourself with winners.

Granted, that is not always as easy as it sounds. For instance, people who are trying to lose weight often live with enablers. Steven wants to lose weight but his wife, Heather, isn't concerned about it. She keeps three or four cartons of ice cream in the freezer at all times. She cooks "Southern style," with plenty of butter and saturated fats, and has bread and sugar-filled desserts at every meal. Heather loves Steven, and her cooking is one of the ways she enjoys expressing that love. She is not willing to make a change in her cooking and eating habits. They are both on heart and diabetes medication, but Heather doesn't see that as a problem.

For lasting, positive change, both Steven and Heather need to make the transformation. Otherwise, Heather is going to literally "love Steven to death."

Seek Support

If you are trying to get off drugs or alcohol, support groups are invaluable. Go to meetings, attend church functions, and put yourself in other positive places where people are not using drugs and alcohol. The beneficial roles of faith and prayer will give you added strength as well. But remember the biblical adage: "Faith without works is dead."

Stay away from the negative playmates and playthings; instead, immerse yourself in the positive. Avoid counterproductive atmospheres where the activities you are trying to overcome are evident. These environments may not be negative for other people, but might be destructive for you. For instance, if you want to overcome alcoholism, avoid meeting your friends in bars. If you are trying to kick drugs, don't hang out in seedy joints where you know drug deals are likely to happen. If you are trying to lose weight, don't hang out at the ice cream parlor.

Set some protective hedges around yourself, some boundaries you can't easily cross, and through which negative influences can't as easily reach you. Over time you will develop the necessary skills to go into any environment and function well, but you cannot do that at first. You must take precautions that will keep you on track with the goals you want to achieve, and by surrounding yourself with winners and the positive elements of the world you are trying to create, you will soon discover that you are enjoying an entirely new quality of life.

QUESTIONS About
SURROUNDING YOURSELF WITH WINNERS

1. An old saying suggests, "Show me your friends and I will show you your future." List three of your friends and describe how they might affect your future positively or negatively.

1. _____

2. _____

3. _____

2. What three qualities do you most admire in another person?

1. _____

2. _____

3. _____

3. In regard to your current situation, where do you see yourself in the stages of change?

_____

_____

_____

_____

4. On a scale of 1 to 10 (10 being excellent), rate how well you are maintaining your primary relationships (e.g., your spouse, children, parents, closest friends).

Your spouse   ____

Your children   ____

Your parents   ____

Your closest friends   ____

Others   ____

5. Who do you know who might be a mentor/role model for you, a person from whom you can learn not merely skills but values? List two or three possibilities, and include each person's contact information. When will you contact these individuals?

1. _____

2. _____

3. _____

PUT YOUR PLAN INTO ACTION

"The greatest room in life," Grandma used to say, "is the room for improvement." We can all do better. Celebrate your past successes, put your failures behind you, and keep moving forward. You must make a plan and put it into action. You won't get it done overnight, but those initial steps are critical. You may not know all that you need or want to know, but you have come to realize the most important element: You know that you must get started.

13

The Game Plan Isn't Optional

Suzanne graduated from college at the top of her class. She was bright, energetic, and excited about getting out into the real world. Jobs were tough to find, though, due to the sluggish economy, so when Suzanne's friend Janeen mentioned that the local factory was hiring, they both made a beeline to the employment office.

"We'll have a blast," Janeen exclaimed. "We'll get our own little apartment on the other side of town and we'll live it up!"

That's exactly what they did. They "lived up" their lives. They worked all week, and partied all weekend, squandering away their wages on drugs and alcohol, as well as wasting their potential, year after year. They always intended to do something significant with their lives, but at age thirty-seven, Suzanne was still working in the factory and living in that same tiny apartment. Janeen had long since gotten married . . . and divorced . . . twice, is still addicted to drugs, and Suzanne is beginning to see the folly of an aimless life.

Through her tears, she said, "I made more plans for the senior prom than I did for the rest of my life! I thought maybe my parents or society or God or *somebody* would plan my life for me. I guess I expected all the pieces of the puzzle to come together by themselves. Looking back, I can see that I didn't even have a proper picture of what the puzzle was supposed to look like."

Some people don't like to make plans or set goals for their futures because it puts too much pressure on them. By not setting goals, however, they are literally abdicating the responsibility for their lives, giving it over to chance. As the old saying goes, by failing to plan, they are planning to fail. Or as J. C. Penney, founder of the department store chain, once said, "Give me a stock clerk with a goal, and I will give you a man who will make history. Give me a man without a goal, and I will give you a stock clerk."

Solid Goals

What are goals, anyhow? A goal is a purpose, an aim, a plan; it is something you expect to do within a certain period of time; in many ways, a goal is a statement of faith, an expression of confidence, and a manifestation of believable hope. More importantly, your goals form the raw materials of your action plan, a concise statement declaring, "This is where I am going and what I want to do, and here is how I'm going to do it."

Driving from my home to my office each day, I often pass a new construction site. Out front of the property is a sign boasting a beautiful artist's rendition of what the finished structure will look like, complete with lovely flowers, shrubs, and robust trees lining the property, even cars in the parking lot. Each time I pass the property, it is interesting to notice the progress and to imagine the process. Somebody had to believe that such a structure was possible, and then visualize how it would look. No doubt, that person surrounded himself or herself with numerous good people who could help get the job done. But with all that, one element was still missing. They needed a plan, some blueprints that showed how the picture could become a reality.

We know to begin building anything without a plan is to welcome waste, inconvenience, and possibly even failure. Yet for some reason, we assume we can transform our lives without a game plan. Believe me, if a blueprint is essential for constructing a building, an action plan for your personal transformation is even more vital to your success. Certainly, you won't accomplish all of your goals overnight, and that's okay. But you need to know where you want to go and how you are going to get there, and you must realize that progress will most likely be measured incrementally, especially in the initial stages of transformation.

> If you do what you have always done, you'll get what you have always gotten.
>
> —*Anonymous*

Regardless of whether you want to overcome an addiction to drugs, alcohol, food, or some other life-controlling issue, establishing an action plan, complete with specific goals, will be critical to your success. Setting specific goals will help you to prioritize and achieve your aspirations.

To be effective, your recovery goals need to be well-formulated, specific, measurable objectives that when accomplished will help you to achieve your dream of living clean, sober, and free. I encourage the setting of short-term goals—steps that can be accomplished each day or week—as well as long-term goals, describing where you want to be in six months, a year, three years, or five years.

> Start by doing what's necessary; then do what's possible; and suddenly you are doing the impossible.
>
> —*St. Francis of Assisi*

I like to use the acronym "SMART" when setting goals. Our goals should be

S = *Specific*—well-defined, so that you know the target at which you are aiming.

M = *Measurable*—so that you can determine your progress as you move toward your goal.

A = *Action-oriented*—so that you know what you plan to do, what it is going to take, and what steps you will take to accomplish your goal.

R = *Realistic*—setting your goal slightly out of reach, but not too far beyond your present capabilities.

T = *Time-bound*—establishing dates in advance for how long it will take to achieve specific goals.

Be Specific

In her one-woman show on Broadway, comedian Lily Tomlin quipped, "I always wanted to be somebody. I see now that I should have been more specific." Lily was right. The first and most important step toward achieving your action plan is to be specific when you are setting your goals. Most people are much too vague about what they want. They are wandering aimlessly and erratically through life—accidents waiting to happen. If they have established any goals at all, they are usually ambiguous or nebulous, nothing that they can actually put any hooks into that will help pull them up the mountain they hope to climb.

Keep in mind, your goals need to be consistent with your new, clean lifestyle that you have visualized. Unfortunately, specific goals can work equally well when they are set upon negative sights. If that is a beer party you are dwelling on, your mental receiver will tune in every time you hear of one. If it is a drug deal you are looking for, you will probably find it. If it is a piece of cake or an improper sexual escapade, your mental GPS will seek it out for you. So make sure your specific goals are aligned with the new life you want to live.

Be Realistic

Some people mistakenly assume that if a big goal is good, a huge goal will be that much better. Not necessarily. Remember, the process of visualization is important in reaching your goals, so if your mind sees in advance that achieving your goal is impossible, it will be. Make sure your goal is realistic. The best goal is the one you place just beyond your current reach, but not beyond your imagination.

For instance, rather than stating a vague and ambiguous goal of "I don't want to be so miserable" or "I'm never going to crave drugs again," a better goal might be, "For the next two weeks, whenever I get down, I will write about my feelings in a journal." This, of course, is a short-term goal, but notice that it is specific, measurable (you will know how much you have written), action-oriented (you are going to *do* something), realistic, and able to be accomplished within a certain period of time. Moreover, you will be able to focus on a healthy behavior rather than dwelling on trying to avoid a negative behavior.

As you work on your action plan, ask yourself some probing questions:

What is my purpose in life?
Where am I going in my life?
What does it look like? Feel like? Sound like?
How will I know when I have gotten there?
Is this activity consistent with my goal, purpose, and plan?
Approximately how long will it take to reach my goal?
What do I regard as important steps along the way?
Who is going to share this adventure with me?
Who can I enlist to help me reach my goals?

Granted, most people never get this specific about their action plan, and of course, that is one of the main reasons they give up on treatment or fail to live their dreams. Your mind needs specific, clearly defined information if you expect your mental computer to help you succeed in reaching your objectives. That's why I suggest that you write down the answers to the above questions as they apply to your physical appearance and health, your family responsibilities, your social life, your education, your financial plans, your professional and career goals, your community activities, and your spiritual life. As you consider each of these areas, ask yourself the hard questions, write out the answers, and keep them someplace where you can review them frequently. It may take a little time to do this exercise, but it will be well worth the investment.

Another exercise that you will find helpful as you consider your game plan is to make a list of your priorities, asking yourself the question: "What really matters?"

A question that helps to sort out your priorities might be as follows: "If you went to the doctor, and he told you that you had only one year left to live, what would you do in the next twelve months?" Your answers to questions such as these will help clarify what you currently regard as priorities. The question you must then ask yourself is, "Are my priorities in alignment with my values and beliefs?"

In establishing a priority list for your goals, it will be helpful to break them down into categories. Start with your long-range, lifetime goals. What do you really want to do with your life? What do you regard as being of highest value to you? Are there some things that you would be willing to sacrifice for? Fight for? Even die for?

You'll find that once you establish your long-term goals, you are much less likely to be absorbed, overcome, or frustrated by the tyranny of the immediate. If you know where you ultimately want to go, you will be less likely to get ensnared or bogged down by things that do not fit into your long-range plans. Ralph Waldo Emerson wisely pointed out, "The world makes way for the man who knows where he is going." On the other hand, as author Robert Mager said, "If you're not sure where you are going, you are liable to end up someplace else."

Write It Down

One of the most important secrets of your success in getting free from addictions or overcoming weight problems will be to write down your goals and your action plan.

I tell people to visualize their future. "Where do you want to live?" I ask them to consider. "Who are the winners with whom you will surround yourself? What type of home and possessions do you have in the new world you are creating? What type of lifestyle do you have?" As they begin to dream, I encourage them, "Good, now write those things down on paper. Keep them in front of you as we move through this process.

"How long is that going to take? What sort of time frame? What is 'success' to you? Clean and sober for a year, five years, thirty years? When you have lost fifty pounds? A hundred pounds? What size are you going to be?

"How are you going to celebrate when you reach your goal? Will you buy yourself some new stylish clothes? Take a special trip?" I encourage that person wanting to change to "define your goal in as much specific detail as possible." It is almost impossible to produce lasting positive change with vague, nebulous, ambiguous plans. You must get specific.

··

**Define your goal in as much specific
detail as possible.**

··

Lifestyle change is similar to opening a new business. Some people open a new business without a business plan, but most of those don't work out very well. If you hope to succeed, your chances are exponentially better if you write out your plan, decide what you want to do, and what it is going to take to bring about success.

You must put your plan on paper. Describe it in detail: What am I trying to accomplish, and how am I going to proceed?

One of the first things I ask someone who wants to change his or her life is "Do you have that on paper? Have you written out your game plan?"

If they haven't written out their game plan—and most have not—I will help them to do so. For instance, at Fit-RX, our weight-loss retreat center, we have a booklet that we ask people to complete, filling out their goals, keeping track of what they eat, noting their weight-loss progress. It is critical to write out the plan, and then you have a guide to follow, even when you are on your own or not with other encouragers.

Plan Long-Term and Short-Term

As you are getting your long-term plan in mind, ask yourself where you want to be twenty years from now. Where do you want to be living? What do you want to be doing? Obviously, this is not going to be a static picture. You will change your long-range game plan from time to time, as you experience new adventures in life and acquire fresh information. Nevertheless, your commitment to living clean, sober, and healthy should not change.

I suggest you do something similar for your five-year goals, your three-year goals, and the life you want to be living next year this time. What do you hope to accomplish regarding your recovery plan within the next twelve months? Write these goals down and keep your action plan in front of you. Do the same for your six-month goals and your one-month action plan. These short-term plans should be consistent stepping-stones toward your long-range goals. If they are not, then reevaluate their importance or, if necessary, adjust your long-term goals.

The most important goals you write down, however, will be your plans for each day. Keep a list of your daily priorities in a notebook, journal, or calendar. At the beginning of each day, write down in a series of short statements your list of things you want to accomplish that day. Carry over things that were not accomplished the day before. Then as you work down through your list of priorities, scratch off or put a check mark by each goal you have completed. Carry leftovers into tomorrow and knock them off first thing in the morning. At first, this process may seem tedious and cumbersome, but with some practice, it will be second nature to you. Furthermore, you will be amazed at how much more you get done each day when you know what it is you want to do.

Revise Regularly

Your goals should be updated on a regular basis. I like to do this along with my wife, Tina, and our children on New Year's Day. It is a great way to start off the new year, and at the same time we can evaluate and see how well we have done in accomplishing our goals over the past year.

Keep in mind that your goals are not ends in themselves. They are a means to an end, stepping-stones to where you want to go in fulfilling your action plan. Human beings are goal-oriented by design. That should give you a hint about life: namely, if you simply concentrate on moving from goal to goal you are going to miss the enjoyment of living. Don't be afraid to stop and smell the roses. Life is more than a group of goals to be attained. It is a journey, not a destination.

Even once you are clean and sober, it is a good practice to continue setting SMART goals, establishing and following a game plan for where you want to go in life.

The Action Plan Works

When I first met Khalil Rafati, he had been addicted to drugs, homeless, penniless, and living on the streets a mere two years earlier, and he still looked rough. His hair hung down to his shoulders, he had holes in his jeans (long before that look was popular), and even more holes in his educational credentials, but I recognized a talent in Khalil. "I'll do anything if I can just work for you at the treatment center in Malibu," Khalil had told Fred Segal. So Fred hired him on the spot. Khalil later said, "I'd heard that the Dalai Lama had meditated up there on those beautiful three hundred acres, and I just wanted to be a part of a place like that."

When Khalil first started with me, he was hired to work the swing shift, and cover for absentee workers or those taking a sick day. The next day, somebody couldn't work, and Khalil got the call. He received another call the following day. Before long, Khalil was working not only full time but overtime as well.

I saw the way Khalil treated our clients, and that he even recommended our facilities to other potential clients. I recognized two qualities in him that are essential in good recovery workers: he had compassion for the clients and a passion for his work. During one of our first conversations, I looked Khalil in the eyes and said, "I want to know more about you." Khalil told me his story, and I hung on every word.

Khalil said, "It felt really good to be acknowledged, and you made me feel good about myself."

Later, when Khalil and I went out to dinner, I told him, "Khalil, you are a talented young man. You are a producer."

What I didn't know was that Khalil's addiction had stemmed from self-loathing, and my simple words of encouragement went straight to his heart. I wasn't flattering him. I honestly recognized something good in Khalil and I acknowledged that in him, and told Khalil that he was gifted.

For somebody with low self-esteem and self-hatred, which is what so much of Khalil's addiction had revolved around—and, indeed, the primary cause of many people's addictions—that sort of affirmation cranked his motor. Instead of telling Khalil what was wrong with him, or scolding him for not living up to his potential, or dealing with him in a condescending, punitive way, I simply told him the truth and tried to encourage him.

Khalil became a walking billboard for our business. He later said, "I got more out of that simple dinner together than all the Tony Robbins material and other motivational seminars I had ever attended."

Before long, Khalil was trained and competent to counsel other alcoholics and substance abusers, including famous Olympic athletes, Grammy Award–winning music artists, hugely successful Hollywood producers, and other high-end clients. How did Khalil reach them? He had empathy for them, not merely sympathy. He understood what it felt like to be addicted and hopeless, regardless of how much money, fame, power, or prestige a person might possess. Khalil knew that deep inside, despite their outward bluster and bombast, many of these celebrity types loathed themselves. Besides sharing his personal story with naked honesty, Khalil genuinely loved his clients, and they responded to his unconditional love—and the hope he represented.

Many of the clients with whom we worked were surprised to be in such a loving, supportive environment. Recovery is a big business nowadays, so all too often, the goal is simply to keep the clients com-ing back and keep the money flowing. But in our program, clients found therapists and counselors who genuinely cared that they get clean and stay clean. Consequently, Khalil's success rate with clients was astronomically high.

I knew that Khalil had made great strides toward overcoming his addictions and helping others to do the same, but I also recognized that he still needed to put in place a specific game plan for his life. I arranged a life-coaching session for Khalil with Greg Montana. Greg taught Khalil about "heart virtue" and encouraged Khalil to set a goal of opening his own business, which I fully supported. I also arranged for Khalil to get some vocational training, fed him good books to read, and helped him establish a one-year plan, as well as a three-year and five-year plan for his life.

Khalil and I worked through a game plan that he could believe in. I didn't allow him to be vague as he visualized his life, but pressed him for specific details. Khalil hedged at first, trying to answer my questions in generalities, but I knew that if I could get him to see and describe where he wanted to go and how he wanted to get there, Khalil could succeed.

"I'm not accustomed to succeeding," Khalil admitted. "Accom-plishing things is not my forte. I'm much better at messing up things and being a failure."

"That's in the past, Khalil," I assured him. "Let's visualize your future and write down your game plan." Repeatedly, I drew Khalil out of ambiguities and toward specific, tangible, measurable goals. "Okay, now what are you going to do about this? How are you going to get there?" I encouraged Khalil to visualize his dream and to specifically review his game plan every day.

I didn't tell Khalil, "Look, you are going to land a rocket on the moon." I told him, "You are going to own your own business." I helped him write out his specific goals, one of which was to open his own intervention business, as well as a juice bar in Malibu. Now that he had been clean for several years, he also wanted to establish a long-term relationship with a woman of character. Khalil heard me talking in glowing terms about my wife, Tina, and he said, "That's the kind of relationship I want with my future wife, too, but Michael, all guys cheat."

"No, Khalil," I responded. "Real men don't cheat on their wives."

"Well, my married friends all cheat," Khalil replied.

"Then you need to make some new friends."

Khalil stared back at me wide-eyed, but he took my words to heart.

"You are going to accomplish all of these things, Khalil," I told him after we went over his one-year, three-year, and five-year plans. "And if you need help at any point, you call me."

Today Khalil owns his own recovery center in California, and is in constant demand with clients. He also owns his own juice bar business in Malibu, just as he had dreamed—and as we had outlined in his game plan. He has traveled all over the world in recent years, has established a long-term relationship with the woman of his dreams, and they plan to marry.

"I'm living my wildest dreams," Khalil says today.

I'm not surprised. And I am equally as confident that you can live your wildest dreams as well, if you will do as Khalil did and write out your game plan as specifically as possible, and then work that plan every day.

14

A Consistent Journey in the Same Direction

Peter Benchley, author of the bestselling book *Jaws*, upon which the blockbuster movies were based, was in Australia observing and filming sharks in their natural habitat. One day, he was standing in chest-deep water just off the shoreline when he spotted a shark approaching him and getting too close for comfort. Benchley turned toward the beach and started running. Although he made it safely to shore, he later commented that trying to run in the chest-high water was like "dancing on peanut butter."

Does that sound like you, or someone you know who is trying to initiate a transformation? Many people are putting in a lot of effort, but don't seem to be making much progress; they are dancing on peanut butter. They are chest-high in water, with the sharks swimming all around them, and yet they can't seem to get moving.

One of Toyota Motor Company's tenets of success is "continuous improvement," linked to the Japanese philosophy of *kaizen*, or "change for the better." Even small improvements are applauded, because wise individuals know that as small changes for the better accumulate, they can yield enormous positive results.

Sometimes we expect change to happen overnight and get disappointed when it doesn't. But real change is often gradual, the accumulation of a large number of small, incremental improvements. So far, we've noticed four key elements to lasting change. First, you have to develop the mindset of believable hope; you must visualize achieving your goals, surround yourself with winners, and put a winning game plan in place—and follow it—doing the hard work to achieve your goals. Success doesn't come easily, but it usually comes to those who are willing to do the right things, to keep taking one step at a time, committed to a long, consistent journey in the right direction. I found this to be especially true when I decided that I needed to lose more than seventy pounds.

Walk Before You Run

When Tina got pregnant with our first child, she put on some extra weight, so as her loving husband, I did my duty and ate for her and me! The good news was she lost her weight after our son, Alex, was born; the bad news was that I kept mine on and added even more. I ballooned seventy to eighty pounds heavier than my normal weight. I was working extra long hours, with lots of stress, and I started eating too much. I knew it was a dangerous combination of factors, which would inevitably take a toll if I didn't change my patterns, yet I continued to ignore the obvious, not willing or ready to make the necessary changes.

I was negotiating to buy an outpatient center in Pasadena from a highly regarded interventionist, Dan Cronin—the owner. He, Darren Kavinoky, a top criminal attorney in California who specializes in DUI cases and other celebrity cases, and I were enjoying a sushi dinner in LA one night when Dan took me by surprise. "You really are fat," he said bluntly.

"What?" Although I knew his reputation as a top-flight interventionist, I was nonetheless stunned by Dan's boldness. "Did you actually say that?"

"Yeah, I'm worried about your health," Dan continued. "You need to get in better shape. You need to lose some weight. Maybe you should start exercising, eating better, and taking better care of yourself. I'm fifty-seven; how old are you?"

"I'm forty."

"Really? You look terrible."

"I'm getting ready to buy your company, Dan. Do you really want to have this conversation?" I looked at Darren for some support, but didn't find it.

Darren looked across the table, shrugged, and said, "But he's right."

Darren knew that blunt honesty is one of Dan's strongest suits. Dan had confronted Darren Kavinoky, a strong personality himself, with a similar boldness a number of years earlier. Dan didn't even recall the incident, but he was attending a party for court personnel when Darren approached him and said, "You probably don't remember me, but you saved my life."

"Really?" Dan's interest was piqued. "Tell me what I did or said, and maybe I'll use it again."

"You were the only person to tell me to shut my mouth and get myself into a bed in a treatment center," Darren said. "So I did. And I'm alive to tell about it today as a result."

One of the leading interventionists in America, Dan Cronin is in constant demand for high-level interventions with celebrity and corporate clients. A former heroin addict, alcoholic, and cancer survivor, who once even survived an airplane crash, Dan is unimpressed with self-pity. When someone tells him, "You don't understand how difficult I've had it in my life," Dan raises his eyebrows and smiles. I knew I wasn't going to be able to convince Dan that my life was stressful, so I had a reason to be overweight.

"I'm just trying to save your life," Dan said to me straightforwardly. We talked further, and Dan encouraged me to start an exercise program. As much as I tried to deflect his statements with humor, the truth of Dan's words seared into my mind. Reality poked a hole in the balloon of my idealism.

I was staying at the Malibu Beach Inn, so when I awakened the next morning around 5:30, I decided, "I'm going to go out and run."

This was a quick business trip; I certainly wasn't planning to include any exercise. I didn't have gym shorts with me so I slipped on a pair of blue jeans. I threw on a T-shirt, laced up my "running shoes," and headed out toward the beach. I took off running down the sand as fast as I could. I hadn't gone more than twenty yards when I began gasping for breath, huffing and puffing like an old man who had smoked cigarettes all his life. I could barely breathe! "I'm going to die!" I said to myself. I pulled up short and tried to calm down. "I'm in terrible shape," I gasped.

I remembered that Grandpa Cartwright was a big man, weighing nearly 300 pounds, and he died of a sudden heart attack at age sixty-four. I recognized that my genes and predispositions were similar to his, so I made a choice. I wanted to live. "I've got to do something about this," I said to myself. "I have to be vigilant if I hope to make it to eighty." Sixty years of age seemed a reach just then. It took all that I could do to struggle back to my room.

When I could finally breathe normally again, around 6:30 in the morning, I called Dan Cronin and cussed him out for goading me into exercising.

"What did you do?" Dan asked.

"I went running like you told me to do."

"Did you start by walking or did you just go running?"

"I ran. I went sprinting down the beach."

"Well, that's the problem," Dan said with a laugh. "Haven't you ever heard the old saying, 'You have to walk before you can run?' Start by just doing some walking every day."

"Oh."

"I'll tell you what. Call me every day, and I'll give you a workout regimen."

About two months later, I celebrated my fortieth birthday. My wife, Tina, gave me a special birthday present—a scale. Not just any scale. Oh, no. This was a high-tech scale that could not only measure my weight but my percentage of body fat, as well as my body "age," and several other depressing factors. The scale said I was in great shape for a man of fifty-four, and whose body fat was horrendous.

I committed myself to getting in shape. I called Dan Cronin, and he walked me through a fitness plan that I could use every day. It was a humbling step, but I needed to do something significant to knock off the weight and reorient my lifestyle around healthy eating and regular exercise. Dan helped me set up an action plan to get my weight under control, and I got serious about watching what I ate. I replaced high-calorie foods with more low-calorie foods such as fruits and vegetables. I cut out all sugar-filled drinks, including sweet tea, sodas, sweetened milks, and coffees, and even juices, many of which are saturated with sugar. Getting rid of my liquid calories was a major deal, as I drank the best energy drink of all—pure water. I read everything I could about the topic of healthy, sustainable weight loss. I began following a daily exercise program, and perhaps most important of all, I established a practice of "journaling" my calorie intake, writing down every bit of food, drink, or condiments that I put in my mouth. By reducing my calorie intake by a mere 500 calories per day, I discovered that I could lose one pound per week, a healthy weight-loss plan. By adding vigorous exercise to my plan, I could burn off even more calories. By following my action plan, my extra pounds disappeared.

Let's Get Radical

I was making good progress getting my weight down, dropping from 230 pounds to about 160 pounds between May and November 2008. From then until April 2009, doing cross-fit exercises, I knocked off another ten pounds and began to build muscle. I enjoyed rediscovering my body shape through an aggressive diet and exercise program, but then, as I often do, I went a bit overboard. After about nine months, I decided to train for a triathlon, so I needed to do something radical to get in even better shape. I searched online and found an "extreme" fitness program in Encinitas, California, known as SEAL-FIT, a fifty-hour, intense physical fitness camp that prepares military members to become Navy SEALs. Designed by a former Navy SEAL, the program looked exciting. I talked my friend Darrin Kavinoky into doing the program with me. At several points, even though I was now in fairly good shape, I questioned the wisdom of my decision.

Neither of us really had a clue what was involved in the rigorous SEALFIT program. We thought we were going away for a weekend camping experience.

When we arrived at the SEALFIT headquarters, we noticed that most of the other participants were between eighteen and twenty years of age and were all in fantastic physical condition. That should have been a hint to us.

At first, Darrin and I looked at each other and panicked, as though wondering, *What in the world did we sign up for?* The trainers were all Navy SEALs or former Navy SEALs instructors. The program was fifty hours of nonstop exercise, including push-ups, sit-ups, running up and down the beach, flutter kicks, running up the hillside, then more of each exercise, then we did a five-mile hike up the mountain. It was nonstop exercise, similar to the Navy SEALs' notorious Hell Week. We ate our MREs (Meals Ready to Eat) in about five minutes. We did each activity to the point of exhaustion, then switched to another exercise or working on another part of the body and did that till we neared the point of exhaustion. We didn't sleep at all during the entire weekend.

Exacerbating matters, twelve hours into the program, my I.T. band snapped in my knee, popping while I was doing an exercise. From that point on, every time I did an exercise, or my leg hit the ground, it felt like a knife slamming into my knee. It was brutally painful.

Mark Devine, the founder of SEALFIT, noticed me grimacing and said, "Here, let me help you out with that." He grabbed my leg and pushed and pulled as hard as he could. Pain seared through me and I wanted to scream. That was enough of that. "I'm good, I'm good!" I bellowed.

"You're fine," Mark said. "You aren't going to die from it. Get back in line."

The excruciating pain in my leg throbbed for the next thirty-eight hours, but I was not about to stop.

By Sunday morning, we were all beat. The instructors herded us into the headquarters hall, where we had a hearty breakfast and then did some yoga-type stretching exercises. We relaxed, feeling that the ordeal was over. Then suddenly, almost without warning, the instructors began throwing water on us, yelling at us to get back out on the beach for more running, more exercises, particularly 100 burpies, vigorous down-and-up exercises.

We were all close to breakdown, but one young man seemed especially ready to crack. He simply could not do the burpies to the satisfaction of the drillmasters. And every time he messed up, all of us suffered, since the burpies we were doing didn't count toward the total unless *everyone* did them correctly in perfect unison. Up and down the beach we went, and not surprisingly, tempers began to flare.

Finally, in the middle of a sprint down the beach, I stopped and waved everyone down, calling the group together. "Come on, guys. Let's do this thing. We're this close. Let's get it together and get it done! Let's finish strong." I led the team through the remaining exercises, and the other guys rallied, even the few slackers, and the guys who were ready to give up. We completed the exercise set to the satisfaction of the drillmasters and finished the course.

At the closing ceremonies, because of my endurance through the pain of my knee, and my rallying the troops near the end of the program, I was given the Fire in the Belly award, voted on by all the leaders and participants. Completing the SEALFIT weekend program gave me incredible confidence that I could do anything I put my mind to, with the proper mental mindset. Think about it: Within nine months, I went from being a pudgy couch potato to receiving an award presented by a Navy SEAL. I was so impressed with SEALFIT that about a year after completing the program, I became a partner in the company!

Healthy Living Becomes a Lifestyle

Nowadays, I work out four times a week. Once in shape, you can have some cheat days, in which you can eat those forbidden pleasures, because your body will continue to burn calories as long as you maintain your workouts. But be careful. Remember, fat cells never disappear; they shrink, but like the monster in a bad B movie, they are lurking, looking for another opportunity to attack. They are still there, ready to fill up again if you tease them with junk food or unhealthy dietary choices.

Healthy eating and regular exercise have now become a lifestyle for me; they are regular parts of my life, as much as brushing my teeth. It is something about which I have to be vigilant for the rest of my life. When I feel myself getting complacent about my eating habits, I go back to what works. I write down every bit of food or drink that I put in my mouth and keep track of my caloric intake.

After facing my own challenge of losing more than seventy pounds at forty years of age, I realized how difficult losing weight really can be. In my earlier years, I had always maintained an active lifestyle, so no matter how poorly I ate, my metabolism burned off most of the excess calories. But as I moved into my late thirties, I found that the pounds didn't disappear as easily. In fact, quite the opposite. All those cakes and pies and potato chips and other junk foods I loved to eat stayed right with me. Getting back to my healthy weight and maintaining it took work and the support of some good friends and mentors.

Out of my compassion for others trying to deal with similar weight-loss issues, I realized the need for an educational, concentrated program similar to our drug and alcohol treatment centers where individuals could find professional help in a luxurious environment, for a week, a month, or as long as it might take to transform their lives. My goal was to make weight management a normal lifestyle choice and to help establish patterns that would be easy to maintain once a person was back home, living on his or her own.

That's how Fit-RX came about. We began by renting a beautiful bed-and-breakfast facility outside Nashville, and outfitting a small gym for workouts and training sessions. We catered to a small number of clients, providing highly personalized care by an elite team of professionals—everyone from dietitians to medical doctors to professional chefs who teach our clients not only how to eat better but how to prepare healthy, tasty food they want to eat. It is a complete program that includes personal diet planning once a person gets back home, as well as nutritional education and fun shopping field trips while on campus. Our success rate with Fit-RX is phenomenal, as our clients learn how to lose weight, look and feel better, and live healthier and more productive lives.

Set Yourself Up for Success

If you are fighting the battle of the bulge, you must stop working against yourself and begin setting yourself up for success. How can you do that? Easy. Start by getting the junk out of your house! Understand, not all fats and carbs are your enemy; some are actually good for you. But trans fats—man-made through a process known as hydrogenation—raise your LDL (bad) cholesterol and lower HDL (good) cholesterol, while increasing inflammation. These fats are deadly enemies and should be avoided in any diet.

Saturated fats, the type derived from animal sources and usually found in meat, butter, and dairy products, were once thought to be the culprits leading to heart disease, but in recent years, these fats have come back into vogue. I'd still enjoy them in moderation, if at all.

Monounsaturated fats, found in almonds, extra-virgin olive oil, avocados, pistachios, and macadamia nuts, are actually beneficial to you, if eaten in small amounts. The calorie content of these fats is high, so if you overdo it on the nuts, you will still put on weight.

Processed carbs, found in most of the processed snacks in your local convenience store, are almost always awful for you.

Why "Diet" Products Are Ineffective

At Fit-RX, we do not recommend fad diets or quick fixes. Managing your weight will take time and commitment. Gimmicks may have their place; appetite suppressants, meal replacement programs, and peer-pressure weight-loss programs all may help. But you must be motivated to change.

Crash diets don't work; quick fixes are disappointing. Lifestyle change is the only sure solution, so commit yourself to a long-term action plan—things you can do and enjoy for the rest of your life—and you will not only reach the weight you desire, but you will maintain it as well.

I like the philosophy of Joy Bauer, the vibrant host of "Joy's Fit Club" on NBC's *Today* show. Joy says, "Life is hard; food should be easy."

The Action Plan Is Not Optional!

What do you believe is possible? Do you actually believe you can lose weight or live without destructive substances? Can you visualize yourself getting free from drugs, alcohol, or the other constraints in your life? Remember: You have to see it before it will happen. Then you must surround yourself with winners, who will encourage you and cheer you onward.

But true transformation also takes accurate knowledge, personal discipline, and most importantly, the execution of your plan. The action plan is not optional! If you want to succeed in any area, it will take concentrated work toward your goals. Whether you want to become a rock star or a rocket scientist, you will have to do the work to achieve your dream. The same is true of transformation. For instance, if you want to lose weight, you can't merely wish the weight away. You can't "think the pounds off," as some popular books purport. Losing weight will require that you develop a good game plan and put it into practice. It's that simple—and it is that hard.

> The three great essentials to achieving anything worthwhile are: first, hard work; second, stick-to-it-iveness; and third, common sense.
>
> —*Thomas Edison*

I meet people all the time who tell me they want to lose weight. "Oh, really?" I'll ask. "How much time are you spending on that?"

"Well, I'm thinking about it." (Sometimes the super-pious will even say something like, "I'm praying about it.")

"Oh, okay. Good luck with that."

We both know that it isn't going to happen if he or she is not willing to put in the time and effort to write out and implement a plan of action to achieve the goal. By failing to write out specific goals, we are planning to fail by default.

Before you begin any extravagant, extraordinary, or expensive weight-loss program, do a bit of research on yourself. For one week, write down in a journal or notebook everything you eat and drink, every day. No cheating now! Almost everything contains some calories, including that can of soda pop (which may actually have a lot of calories) to the orange juice you had at breakfast to the quick doughnut you had with a cup of coffee during your break at work. It is not simply the big meals we have to keep under control; when you want to lose weight, every calorie counts!

Even many of the things that "sound" healthy or nutritious are loaded with sugar and fat. For instance, that granola bar that advertisers hype as being "good for you" is laced with sugar and fat. It might take you as much as forty-five minutes of walking a treadmill or swimming to work off the effects of that one granola bar. Other seductively healthy-sounding foods are equally deceptive. Yes, carrot cake does contain carrots, but one slice of carrot cake can be anywhere from 600 to 1,000 calories! True, spaghetti or any sort of pasta can be a healthy choice, but not if you smother it in creamy, fat-filled sauces. And that blueberry muffin in the morning? If you enjoy it, eat it, but don't kid yourself. It is mostly cake with a couple of blueberries—it certainly wouldn't qualify as your minimum fruit requirement for the day. You'd be better off to have a banana or some fruit salad. Drinks count, too, when you begin to seriously consider what you are putting in your mouth. That grande latte can have as many or more calories as a sugar-loaded candy bar.

So begin by keeping track of all of the meals, snacks, and drinks you ingest this week. List everything with calories that you swallow, whether solid or liquid (that glass of orange juice probably has around 100 calories). Then look up the calorie content and write it down next to the item you are eating or drinking. Remember, very few items other than water, tea, and coffee have no calories; some like celery are quite low, but still have some caloric content. Write it down. Now ask yourself, "Is it physically possible to lose weight eating and drinking these things?" Your metabolic rate can be obtained from your physician and at many fitness centers. It isn't difficult information to gather. But it is vital to know what your body needs, and what kind of energy you burn each day, if you want to lose weight.

The more accurately you write down your caloric intake, compared to your metabolic rate, the more you will realize how far off the mark you are currently, and how important it is to make some changes. *Yikes! I'm taking in more than 3,500 calories every day and my metabolic rate is only 2,000, so I'm on track to gain half a pound every week!*

That doesn't sound like much, until you realize that half pound per week turns into twenty-six pounds per year. At that rate, in five years, you would be putting on 130 pounds! That is in addition to what you weigh right now!

> We are what we repeatedly do. Excellence, then, is not an act, but a habit.
>
> —*Aristotle*

No doubt you've often heard someone like Sheila, who tells all her close friends, "I want to lose some weight." Sheila seems to think that merely saying the words will get the job done. She doesn't do any of the homework to find out the calorie value of the foods and drinks she is taking into her body. She doesn't get specific about a game plan to lose weight, and she fails to write down any plan that she dreams up in her mind. Not surprisingly, Sheila has yet to lose the first pound.

Sheila's lack of a plan is not unusual. Few people who are not in a weight-loss program actually write down their calorie intake compared to their metabolic rate, the rate at which their bodies will burn off calories. You can't deal in vague generalities if you honestly hope to lose weight. You must deal in hard facts and have a written game plan.

On the other hand, Steven developed a written plan of action to lose weight. He said, "My body weight is currently 225 pounds. I want to be 165 pounds, and I want to be at that weight in nine months. To do that, I need to lose six and two-thirds pounds every month, which is approximately one and two-thirds pounds each week, so my calorie intake needs to be X per day if my metabolic rate is Y." He got that specific, put it all down on paper, and then laid out a plan to lose the weight. Sure enough, nine months later, Steven was enjoying his lean, healthy, 165-pound body.

Come up with a game plan, both to eliminate the negative input and to embrace those things that will help you. Establish a specific, detailed plan of what you want to achieve and then follow through! Change your mindset by telling yourself, *I'm going to do it; this is how I'm going to do it. This is the team I am putting in place to help me. This is the environment I want to stay in. I am going to stay away from fast-food restaurants; I'm going to tell Larry that I'm not going with him to that restaurant that features huge portions and fattening cheesecake. I'm going to take my lunch to work—packing a grilled chicken breast and an apple instead of a large portion of pasta—rather than going out to fast-*

food restaurants every day. Those are the kinds of statements—not to someone else but to yourself—that will help you change your mindset. And when you change your mindset, you can change your life!

Here's How It Works

Growing up in Florence, South Carolina, with her daddy a music minister and her family active at the Baptist church, Bree Boyce, Miss South Carolina 2011, found overeating to be one of the more acceptable vices. Although her mom and dad were slim, and her siblings were blessed with metabolisms that burned calories away, Bree's body created fat cells almost by looking at food. "I was the 'lucky' one," Bree quips today. "My sister, size double zero, could eat a huge piece of chocolate cake, and it wouldn't affect her. If I had a chocolate chip cookie, it stayed with me."

By the age of seven, Bree's cute, cherubic chubbiness was becoming a problem. "I started gaining the weight gradually after age seven, and just kept increasing." It wasn't that Bree didn't enjoy healthy fruits and vegetables; she liked junk food better. As her weight went up, her self-esteem went down. She felt terrible about herself. Entering her teen years, when most of her friends were going to dances and swimming parties, Bree became more self-conscious about her body, but rather than changing her eating habits and becoming more physically active, she became more reclusive, camping out in front of the television for hours on end and pigging out on junk-food snacks. She looked to food for comfort rather than fuel.

At school, Bree played the role of "the funny fat girl," poking fun at herself, joking about her weight in an effort to fit in with her peers, encouraging her companions to laugh at her expense. All the while, inwardly Bree's heart was breaking. She had so many lofty dreams—

she wanted to go to college, sing on Broadway, get married, and have a family—and none of that seemed possible as her weight continued to escalate.

By age sixteen, Bree's weight had bloated to more than 200 pounds. She experimented with fad weight-loss programs and low-carb diets, all to no avail. She tried working out with a trainer, but then as soon as she finished the workout, she'd drive from one fast-food restaurant to another, usually gulping the food down quickly in the car so nobody would see her cheating.

But her weight problem was impossible to hide. By seventeen, Bree's weight ballooned to 234 pounds; she wore size 18 jeans and extra-extra-large clothing. Her knees were giving out due to the excess weight she was carrying, and she needed an inhaler to breathe.

"Despite my condition," Bree told me, "I avoided going to the doctor. I knew they would put me on a scale and weigh me."

Bree's expectations were correct. What she did not expect, however, was the doctor's frank and frightening assessment. "He looked me in the eyes and said, 'It is time for you to lose the weight, because if you don't, your knees will be unable to carry you.'"

Okay, Bree thought. *So my knees won't work. I can handle that.*

But the doctor was not done with his diagnosis. "If you don't lose weight, Bree," he paused momentarily, as though he really didn't want to continue, "you're going to die." He handed the overweight teenager a handicap parking sticker.

That was Bree's wake-up call, the moment when the light turned on in her heart and mind. That very day, she committed herself to rediscovering the person she had been created to be.

Changing her diet wasn't easy, especially since her entire family ate poorly, but Bree determined that she would start the process by establishing an action plan, setting reasonable short-term goals. She began simple exercises two to three times a week, kept track of the food she ate, and set a goal of losing five pounds within a month. When she weighed herself four weeks later, she was thrilled. She had lost seven pounds!

That victory spurred her onward.

Although she had made a start, the change was by no means overnight. But Bree kept working her action plan. Meanwhile, she knew that people made fun of her because of her weight. Dating was difficult if not downright out of the question. The young man who invited Bree to the prom stood her up because his friends teased and picked on him so badly for wanting to take her to the dance. Bree was devastated, but the insult inspired her even more.

She continued working at her weight loss. At first, she was on her own, so she joined a gym. But Bree's family members soon joined in the fight. As part of their game plan for success, they consulted with a nutritionist, cut out all junk foods and processed foods, drank water instead of sodas or sugar-filled juices, and wrote down everything they ate. Even Bree's slim and trim family members were shocked when they discovered from their food journals that they had been consuming more than 3,000 calories each day. Fruits and vegetables became staples around the Boyce home. In the process, not only did Bree lose weight, but her mom was able to get off all medication for high cholesterol as well.

Bree's workout regimen was anything but a piece of cake. She exercised as much as three hours each day. She attended Zumba dance classes and began walking or jogging every day of the week. At times she got discouraged at the slow pace of progress. "Please help me, God," she prayed. "I just don't think I can do this anymore."

In those moments, Bree said later, "It was almost as though a still, small voice spoke to me inside, saying, 'Keep going. Tomorrow is a new day. You can do it. I will help you.' My faith definitely helped." It took three years, but Bree dropped an astonishing 112 pounds! She went from a size 18 to a size 2.

While some people may joke that they are half the man or woman they used to be, Bree actually is. "I look in the mirror and realize that I lost an entire *me*!" she says, her eyes sparkling with joy.

With her self-confidence soaring, Bree entered the Miss South Carolina pageant and won, qualifying her for the Miss America pageant. She maintained her normal schedule of working out for three hours each day in preparation, but then in September 2011, only a few months before the nationally televised pageant, Bree suffered a serious setback.

While at an outdoor exercise class, Bree and the group were doing box jumps, a vertical jump from the ground to the top of a box, and back down. There were more participants than boxes, so Bree offered to use a brick wall surrounding a flower bed as her box. During one of her leaps up and down off the wall, Bree missed. She slammed into the brick wall shins first on the edge of the brick, slicing both of her legs wide open, all the way to the bone. It took more than one hundred stitches to sew the skin on Bree's shins back together. For the next three weeks, crucial pageant preparation time, she couldn't walk without crutches or a walker. And of course she couldn't work out.

With her skin sewn together, her dreams of being Miss America dashed against a brick wall, it would have been easy for Bree Boyce to have turned back to food for comfort. She didn't. Instead, she had her family members bring her some weights and she continued to work on her upper body while her legs recovered.

She was uncertain whether she would be able to walk normally, much less in high heels on the notoriously slick Miss America stage. But Bree was determined to represent her state, her family, and herself at the pageant. She didn't win the Miss America crown, but she won the hearts of everyone who met her.

Today, Bree enjoys being active and maintains her fit figure by eating a healthy diet, exercising every day of the week, and avoiding the junk food that she formerly craved. "One person asked me, 'Do you mean you don't ever eat any of the foods you love?' and I said, 'No, I'm eating the foods I enjoy. I'm just not eating such large portions, and I'm not eating junk food. It is a lifestyle for me. If I have a piece of cake, I don't feel guilty. I know that in moderation, those kinds of foods are okay, but when I eat something bad, I can feel the difference in my body. So if I have a piece of cake today, it will be small. And I won't have a piece tomorrow."

Today, Bree is spreading the word about healthy eating and exercising, especially to teenagers. She's happy being the best Bree that she can be. "It's not about the number on the scale," she says, "it is about being healthy. You can be slim, and still be eating poorly and not getting the nutrition your body needs." Nor should you compare yourself to others. Bree says, "It is about finding that beautiful person you were created to be."

Oh, and what about that fellow who stood up Bree for her high school prom? They hadn't seen each other since high school, but a few days after Bree won the title of Miss South Carolina, she returned to her hometown, a gorgeous, trim, 119-pound beauty queen, and she happened to bump into the guy who had jilted her.

His eyes agape, the cad was nearly speechless. "He said, 'Hey,'" Bree recalled with a laugh, "but it was kind of a 'hey' with a stutter. He didn't have much to say."

God does have a sense of humor.

Bree Boyce put a plan of action into place, and she is reaping the rewards today, and helping a lot of other people as well.

If You Want Some Help

Amazingly, many people who enter our programs *cannot* establish a weight-loss plan on their own, much less develop a mindset that allows them to believe they can actually lose weight. They can't do it on their own. They can't get specific about their goals. They won't write out a plan and follow it. They don't know what the measurements are, much less the goals they hope to achieve. Often, they have a mental or emotional issue that works against them. Somebody abused them as a child, or someone heaped horrible negative input in their mental computers. Now they simply cannot see themselves as healthy. Maybe they have tried before and failed. Perhaps they are too willing to fudge on their figures when they are trying to keep track of what they really take into their mouths. Possibly they have developed such negative self-concepts, they genuinely see themselves as perpetually overweight. But all of that can change when we allow our mindsets to be transformed!

That's where we start. At Fit-RX, one of the divisions of American Addiction Centers, we help that person to visualize the life he or she wants, to see it, believe it, and develop a plan to succeed. If you go through the process of visualizing your success, writing a specific, detailed plan for what you want to do and how you are going to do it, and then following through with the baby steps in the right direction, you are almost guaranteed success.

It is astounding what an ordinary person can accomplish, once his or her mindset has been redirected toward his or her goals. William showed up at SEALFIT, the rigorous fitness program designed to help men qualify to become Navy SEALs. Of course, many people who go through the program simply want to improve their physical fitness, but William aspired to become a SEAL.

But there was a problem. I practically had to carry William through camp. *How is he ever going to make it through real SEAL training?* I wondered. But a year later, William qualified as a Navy SEAL. He attributed his success to the SEALFIT camp. "I never realized that it was mental toughness that I needed to develop," said William. "I could handle the physical training, but the mental toughness was something I lacked. It's all about not quitting, doing the work, day in and day out, taking another step when you are exhausted, doing one more pushup when your arms are burning, that sort of thing."

Once your mindset is adjusted, you don't dare sit back and relax. Quite the contrary, you have to put in the hard work. No one becomes the best at anything by coasting. Malcolm Gladwell reminds us in his book *Outliers* that most people who are huge success stories, whether you are talking about Bill Gates, the founder of Microsoft, or the Beatles, have put in more than 10,000 hours practicing, preparing, exercising their skills before they became successful. Their success wasn't accidental, serendipitous, or even providential. It was the result of "grunt it out" work over a long period of time.

The Sunday before Mother's Day 2011, President Barack Obama went on national television to announce that nearly ten years after 9/11, Osama bin Laden was dead. When more information came out regarding the details of how the man who launched the devastating attacks against America had been killed, the world was in awe that a group of Navy SEALs could pull off the impossible—raiding bin Laden's compound in Pakistan and bringing the leader of al-Qaeda to justice.

People who know about Navy SEALs, however, were not surprised. These guys are the best. The Navy SEALs who killed bin Laden probably put years of brutal effort into their training. We're talking about kick-you-in-the-butt training, getting up at 5:00 a.m., going on ten-mile marches while carrying sixty-pound backpacks, then coming back and doing three hours of calisthenics. They spend hundreds of hours on the firing range, honing their skills as sharpshooters. They practice jumping out of planes for years, going over every move again and again, making sure they are prepared. They perform like Cyborg fighting machines in some science fiction movie, yet in actuality, they are simply young men who have been willing to pay the price in their hearts and minds as well as their physical bodies to be the best in the world. And they are!

If you really want your life to change, it will take a similar level of commitment on your part. You have to want it, but if you are willing to do the hard work required in true transformation, you can have believable hope that your dreams can be turned into reality.

The Untold Secret of Transformation

If you have the best game plan for external change, but ignore the emotional healing that needs to accompany it, your outward transformation will most likely be temporary. You will subconsciously slip back into the emotions that lead to negative behaviors. This explains why someone will lose weight and gain again, yo-yo fashion. For real, lasting change, you need an emotional healing game plan as well. This involves the change of mindset.

Certainly, life's circumstances have an impact: Stress and other emotional issues often lead to overeating, or attempts to drown our sorrows with alcohol or drugs or food. We're trying to stuff the pain by stuffing our faces, and even though we know better, we allow the problem to control us. For instance, Ann Claire, an attractive friend of our family, went through a difficult divorce and immediately began putting on weight.

Tina and I invited Ann Claire and her children to join us on vacation with our family shortly after Ann Claire's divorce. We talked compassionately but honestly about Ann Claire's weight. Understand, she was not 500 pounds, but she was seriously overweight for a woman her size, and her weight was moving in the wrong direction (to say nothing of her mindset).

"I've done this before," Ann Claire admitted, "allowing my weight to get away from me, but something has always clicked in, causing me to get back to eating right and exercising regularly and getting myself back in good shape. This time, nothing is working. It just hasn't clicked."

I understood what Ann Claire was saying, and could empathize with her. She wasn't merely dealing with weight issues; she was stressed and depressed. Her entire screen through which she viewed life had been decimated, and she needed a renewed mindset.

"You already know what to do," I tried to encourage her. "You know what exercises work for you and how to eat, and how to put your plan together."

I knew that Ann Claire possessed a great deal of knowledge about calorie intake, the number of calories in various foods, and how to burn them off, so I was baffled as to why her regimen wasn't working. She had all the usual excuses—too busy, too fatigued, too broke, too discouraged.

Ann Claire knew that overcoming her busy life was simply a matter of schedule and priorities, getting up an hour earlier to take a walk or scheduling time at the gym or a bike ride in the evening. She knew how to vary her exercise program to keep it from becoming boring, changing her exercise from simply time in a gym to more interesting outside activities such as skiing, tennis, swimming, dance, and other choices she enjoyed. Even her tired, aching body could be rejuvenated, she knew, by simple exercises that would stimulate more energy, strengthen her muscles and joints, and help keep her bones strong.

And although her financial status had changed drastically since her divorce—women often suffer more long-term financial devastation than men who divorce—she still could afford a modest exercise program in her budget. Ann Claire also knew better than to compare herself to others. In fact, Ann Claire knew as much about diet and exercise programs as many trainers.

Yet something was missing.

Ann Claire did not need more knowledge; she needed believable hope, the mental mindset that would make use of the information she already possessed and help her put together a game plan to get back on track.

While on vacation, Ann Claire was trying to start over by reestablishing her exercise routines, running on the beach and doing simple exercises. But I noticed Ann Claire's actions—she was still drinking several sugar-filled soft drinks every day, eating ice cream and other junk foods. Even a good workout burns off only about 500 calories, and a few scoops of ice cream can negate all that effort in a matter of minutes.

Finally, I gently confronted Ann Claire about the inconsistency of her actions and attitudes. "Ann Claire, I can help you put together a great game plan for managing your weight, but until you deal with the emotional issues, you will always have a struggle."

"What do you mean?" she asked.

"Ann Claire, real transformation is ninety percent mental. You have all the formulas for good diet and exercise, but we need to work on your mindset, to help you overcome the mental part, so you can begin to see yourself as healthy again. Let's get you in therapy and start visualizing the behavioral changes you want to make."

Ann Claire's face brightened, and for the first time in months, she seemed confident that she could do it.

Look Inside

An important step toward changing your mindset is admitting that there is an emotional issue. For instance, most people who go to a gym hoping to lose weight rarely consider, "I need to look at what's going on in me internally, mentally and emotionally." That doesn't even show up on their radars. They are ready to buy the latest membership or buy a new exercise machine, or some mysterious body-building pill or potion, but they leave out the mental side, which is 90 percent of all transformation.

When you feel beaten down and defeated, it sometimes takes radical action to shuck off the shackles that have held you in place for so long. It is not easy to overcome the effects of the trauma that has affected you. But you owe it to yourself to start. For example, it is difficult to heal when you allow yourself to remain entangled in a toxic environment. Perhaps you need to move out, or move on.

But you don't need to move across the country to change your environment. Sometimes moving across town may be equally effective. Oftentimes, extricating yourself from an unhealthy relationship can be a first step in a positive direction.

More frequently, the real changes need to take place within the environment in which you live. For instance, I suggested to Ann

Claire that she needed to change her environment by cleaning out all the processed foods in her house. As long as there are potato chips and candy and ice cream and other high-sugar, high-carb, high-calorie items in her pantry or refrigerator, the temptation will always be there. "Oh, one candy bar won't really hurt." Getting rid of those items and replacing them with fruit or healthy snacks will be a major change for her, but will greatly improve her chances of success in making the lifestyle changes she wants to maintain.

No More Excuses!

Everyone has experienced something that could cause a negative response to life, spawning a destructive lifestyle. But you do not need to keep reliving past pain, holding on to resentments, or blaming other people for your current condition.

The big question for most of us is not "Can I change for the better?" Of course, we can change! I believe you can change; in fact, I *know* you can transform your life. But the pivotal question is, "Do *you* want to change?" Do you *want* to feel better, look better, and live better? What I want for you, or what your spouse wants, or what other people want for you is almost irrelevant. What matters most is, do you genuinely wish to become a healthy, whole person, or would you prefer to continue life emotionally and physically handicapped by your own self-imposed limitations? It is almost unbelievable how many people will hang on so tenaciously to drugs, alcohol, food, or something else that is making them sick, turning their lives upside down, and destroying their hope for a better tomorrow. Although they talk a great deal about wanting to be well, they continue to clutch on to their physical and emotional crutches. Many people who live with life-controlling issues have gotten to the point where they cannot get free without help, but the good news is that today, help is available.

Most of us have enough head knowledge to be well. We know what we ought to do; we've been inundated by a plethora of books, audio-visual materials, and self-help aids. If you are looking for information or answers to your questions, you'll have little trouble finding them.

Nor is there a dearth of competent counselors, educational resources, or even financial assistance either publicly or through insurance programs (although some insurance plans do not yet cover weight loss, but most soon will). All these issues are superfluous. The real question is: Do you want to transform your life?

If you do, then it is time to get rid of your excuses. What are some of the excuses you might have for remaining in your current condition? Let me guess a few.

Procrastination

When you ask most people, especially those you know who are struggling with life-controlling issues, "Do you want to change?" you expect them to say, "Yes, of course, I want to change. I've been down in the dirt for so long. I'm tired of this kind of life. I don't want to live this way any longer."

That's what you and I would say, right?

Unfortunately, many people are terrible procrastinators. "I'm waiting," they say. "Waiting for the right time. One of these days, I'm going to change, but not yet. Not right now." They almost give the impression that they want you to pat them on the back because they recognize they are not making progress and they are stuck in a rut. "I want to deal with my addiction," or "I'm going to start living up to my potential," or "I'm going to enroll in a weight-loss program and start attaining some of my goals . . . soon. But not today. I'm not ready. I'll start *tomorrow*."

You and I know that tomorrow never comes. And if you wait until you are absolutely ready to begin your action plan, you may never get there. How many miserable old bachelors do you know who decided to wait until they were *ready* before they got married? How many people do you know who say, "One of these days, when I get good and ready, I'm going to straighten out my life"? Think back for a moment on the stages of change we considered previously, and you can see that many people around us remain in those precontemplative and contemplative stages, assuming that one day, life will change for the better.

It can. But one of the prerequisites to changing your mindset is to drop your excuses and stop procrastinating. As a popular Nike running shoe commercial said, "Just do it."

I've Tried Before and Failed

Of course, you have! And so have I. And so has everyone else you know. But as we noted in a previous chapter, relapse is normal! We all fall down, but we don't have to stay down. Anyone who is a success at anything has experienced failure, slipups, letdowns, and discouragements. The key to transformation is to stick with it. Don't allow your mind to dwell on negatives, whether they are personal setbacks or situations over which you have no control. Keep your mindset positive, believing that you will accomplish your goals.

Other People

This is a common excuse for almost any aberrant behavior: It is somebody else's fault. "Other people set me up," or "Other people let me down." Does that sound like you, or someone you are trying to help? "I really want to change, but other people keep messing with me." Or perhaps the excuse is turned around: "I don't have anyone to help me, so I relapse easily." All too often we blame other people for our own failures. "I was doing great until I bumped into Dana. She invited me to a party, and even though I knew it was not a good place for me, I went. It's her fault."

What a wonderful world it would be if it wasn't for all those *other people*!

In Nashville, we have many brilliant music artists, some of whom are quite eccentric. One particular fellow is a musical genius, a veritable fountain of creative ideas, a man whose abilities have been recognized and honored throughout the professional music industry. It is doubtful, however, that you will see him appearing on one of the annual music awards shows. Unfortunately, he is paranoid and doesn't like to be around other people in his industry. He feels that they have all done him dirty, or would if they could. He is certain that somebody is out to get him.

Consequently, he refuses to take part in any of the promotional activities that could enhance his career. He is convinced that he has been victimized by the system. Other people have used him, abused him, and taken advantage of him. People in whom he had placed his trust have disappointed him. He has been burned before, and he is not going to stick his neck out again.

If that sounds like you, you need to realize that *everybody* has been let down by somebody. Furthermore, every one of us has disappointed someone else at some point in our lives. It is counterproductive to complain, "My husband let me down," or "My wife disappointed me," or "My best friend betrayed me."

"And that's the reason I am an addict. That's the reason why I eat so much, drink so much, hoard items for which I have no use, spend long hours viewing pornography, or gamble away my life's savings."

Each of us is accountable for our own actions and our own responses to the actions of other people. You may not be able to control what other people say about you, or do to you, but you alone decide how you will react to adversity or opposition. You can clam up in a shell, you can seal yourself off in your own gloom and despair, or you can choose to move past the pain and disappointment and live out your new positive mindset.

I'm Inferior

Another common excuse is, "I just can't do it. I don't have what it takes. I'm not as strong [or as intelligent, attractive, rich, or whatever] as others. It's not that I don't want to change. Honest, I do. I'm just not able. I know my place in life. This is who I am. I've always been an alcoholic, and always will be. I'm just a junkie looking for my next hit. I want to get a good job and get ahead in life, but I'm not as talented as those folks. I don't have the necessary skills so my career has passed me by. The people who are in treatment are able to afford it; I can't. That person who has overcome her food addiction and is now enjoying a vibrant social life . . . she's much prettier than I am. Look at her body shape. She's naturally beautiful. Not me. I don't have the physical attributes; I don't have the mental acumen. When the gifts were passed out, I didn't get any."

It is easy to make excuses for our failures, and to acknowledge our own inferiority sounds almost noble. But it is still an excuse for not living life to the fullest.

Okay, so your father was an alcoholic or your mother suffered from depression. You may have predispositions toward alcohol abuse or depression or both, but you can overcome those things with proper treatment and a new mindset.

And yes, you've been hurt. We've all been hurt, and we've all hurt other people. But no good will come from continuing to let the past destroy your future.

Don Henley and the Eagles' song "Get Over It" offers good advice, but the big question is "How? How can I move forward?" That's where your action plan really comes into play. It is critical that you commit to doing whatever it takes to get free; you will put your action plan together and start moving forward.

> We can't solve problems by using the same kind of thinking we used when we created them.
>
> —*Albert Einstein*

The Stigmas Are Gone

In July 1987, Kitty Dukakis, wife of then Massachusetts governor Michael Dukakis, a candidate for president of the United States in 1988, came out openly and announced that she had been treated successfully for a secret twenty-six-year addiction to amphetamines—"speed." She spoke candidly about receiving treatment for her addiction at Hazelden Clinic in 1982. When the news broke, some people recoiled at the thought that a potential First Lady of the United States would be a former drug user, but most people hailed Mrs. Dukakis as a hero for honestly admitting what millions of other women endured privately. "I am now drug-free and I have been for five years," she told an audience. "I'm very proud of that. . . . I am telling my story because I want to help others."

Mrs. Dukakis later wrote a book, *Now You Know*, revealing how her addiction began with diet pills and spiraled downward, and was exacerbated by her alcoholism and intense insecurity, depression, and mental illness. In the opening to her book, she admitted, "Had my husband been elected to the highest office in the land in 1988, it could have been very dangerous for me. At the time of the presidential campaign, I was addicted to alcohol. Had the vote gone differently, had Michael and I moved into 1600 Pennsylvania Avenue, I am certain the first crisis would have sent me out of control. I am equally certain, thrust into the smothering, protective confines of the White House, I would not have been able to seek proper help."

Interestingly, Kitty Dukakis was not a sopping drunk. Usually, she would have only one drink. "After an exhausting day's work, my road staff and I would board the plane. Marlene Dunneman, the flight attendant, would have drinks ready. For most of us, vodka was the beverage of choice and our airborne happy hour commenced when we flew off to the next stop. As I said, before I always had one drink.

"One drink."

"Oh, but I thought about that one drink constantly. One drink, and I spent hours picturing it being poured. I could feel the glass in my hand, imagine the cold liquid sliding down my throat . . . And while I didn't actually stiff-arm my drink, I would drain the contents far more quickly than anyone else. I'd finish and then look around at the others who were still sipping. I felt guilty, so awfully guilty, and ashamed. I wanted another, yet, I knew I shouldn't ask for more. I could not afford to; I had work to do and an image to maintain. Moreover, I didn't want my staff to know how much I needed that pick-me-up. I didn't even want to know myself."[11]

When I heard her story, I knew others could identify with her dilemma, so at one of our first addiction conferences, I invited Mrs. Dukakis as a keynote speaker. With her open, warmhearted admissions, she reminded her listeners that the stigmas about seeking help for addictions were gone.

Years later, I talked with a woman about her weight-loss issues and suggested that she get into one of our residential therapy facilities. "Oh," she said. "I could never afford to do that."

"You can't afford it?" I asked, fully aware that she lived in a beautiful home in one of the most prestigious and expensive sections of her city.

"Well, I guess I *can* afford it," she said. "I just wouldn't want my friends to know that I was in therapy." We were getting down to the real reason for her reluctance, so we talked about the fact that most people nowadays don't look down on someone who has sought help.

Most of the stigmas once associated with drug and alcohol rehabilitation centers have long since disappeared. A similar phenomenon has happened with weight loss as well, thanks to some celebrities openly admitting their battles with the bulges, and their willingness to seek treatment. First Lady Michelle Obama also helped shine the spotlight on the need for better diets in our schools. If there were once negative consequences associated with residential treatment centers, those issues have disappeared. We no longer have that excuse.

Regardless of the transformation you hope to achieve, write out your action plan and commit yourself to taking away the excuses for not doing it!

But I Travel a Lot

Bart claimed that he wanted to lose weight, and he blamed his poor eating habits and lack of exercise on the fact that he was a sales representative for a major company. "My job requires me to be on the road," he said, "staying at hotels and eating out at restaurants." His mindset was that he was doomed to a poor diet, that weight loss for him couldn't be done.

Bart came back to his hotel room around 8:30 p.m. after a long, busy day meeting with clients. He was hungry from not having eaten all day. "I'm too tired to exercise," Bart said, "so I think I'll just order room service and watch a movie on television." He dialed the hotel restaurant and even ordered a semi-healthy meal. When his food arrived, Bart turned on the movie and scarfed down his late-night dinner. Still hungry, Bart dialed room service again and ordered the Death by Chocolate cake, with two scoops of vanilla ice cream.

The reason Bart is overweight has nothing to do with his being a sales representative. It has everything to do with his eating habits and lack of exercise. Most of the hotels where he stays have gyms or small workout rooms. He could go out to a grocery store when he arrives in town and buy some fruit, rather than be tempted by the tantalizing desserts at restaurants. A twenty-minute workout of five push-ups, ten sit-ups, and fifteen squats done repeatedly could burn more than 400 calories every night right in his hotel room. He could walk or run around his hotel or swim laps in the pool.

At the restaurants, he could order chicken or fish, without all the fattening sauces. For breakfast, he could eat boiled eggs, oatmeal with cinnamon, or fruit.

It isn't always easy to maintain a healthy diet and exercise program on the road, but it can be done. It requires a change of mindset, changing to an attitude of believable hope rather than making excuses for laziness or lack of personal discipline. It may be more challenging than lying in bed gulping down burgers and fries, but it is worth it.

Put your game plan into practice, and remember: No more excuses!

It Is a Lifelong Process

Over the winter of 2011, my wife, Tina, said, "Michael, you're really eating poorly again."

I was working out regularly at the time, so I said, "It's not affecting me."

But by springtime, my poor diet habits had started to catch up with me. I knew I had to get my mindset dialed back in to a healthy eating regimen, as well as a rigorous exercise plan.

Making the emotional decision to do the right things is the toughest part. Looking back, I analyzed why I allowed myself to slip back into unhealthy eating habits, and I discovered that much of it was due to stress. I had taken on a number of major new business ventures, and had revisited my old eating habits. I had to work my way through a process, asking myself, *Okay, what's really going on here, and why are you eating like that?* I knew better. But I was medicating my high stress levels with comfort food. Not a good plan.

I had to find other ways to relieve the stress in my life. I found some physical activities that were good stress relievers. I also set up several treats—family vacations to lovely resorts—as rewards for my business venture stress. I also made some practical business moves, so that my entrepreneurial efforts did not jeopardize our family's security.

When you see yourself slipping back into old patterns, don't ignore the warning signs. Otherwise, you can find yourself moving in the wrong direction in your transformational process. But here's the good news: You are not alone, and relapses are a normal part of transformation. The question is: How will you respond to a slipup? Part of maintaining believable hope is knowing that relapses can be overcome. In the next section, I'll show you how.

QUESTIONS About
PUTTING YOUR PLAN INTO ACTION

1. Write several of your SMART goals (specific, measurable, action-oriented, realistic, and time-bound) that you are making part of the game plan for your future.

Short-term goals (this week, the next six months, one-year goals):

1. _____

2. _____

3. _____

4. _____

Long-term goals:

1. _____

2. _____

3. _____

4. _____

How will you know when you have achieved the goals in your game plan?

_____

_____

_____

_____

2. What are some small steps you can take immediately to set yourself up for success?

_____

_____

_____

_____

3. How much time will you spend on your Action Plan this week? For the next seven days, list the times and places in which you will work on your action plan.

Day 1 _____

_____

Day 2 _____

_____

Day 3 _____

_____

Day 4 _____

_____

Day 5 _____

_____

Day 6 _____

_____

Day 7 _____

_____

4. What excuses have you used in the past to rationalize your life-controlling issues?

_____

_____

_____

_____

5. How will you overcome those excuses and implement your action plan now that you have believable hope?

_____

_____

_____

_____

Essential Element #5

MAINTAIN THE LIFE YOU LOVE

Ralph Waldo Emerson said, "What lies behind us and what lies before us are tiny matters compared to what lies within us." You may have slipped up in the past, and the future may seem daunting, but you have within you what it takes to maintain the desired transformation.

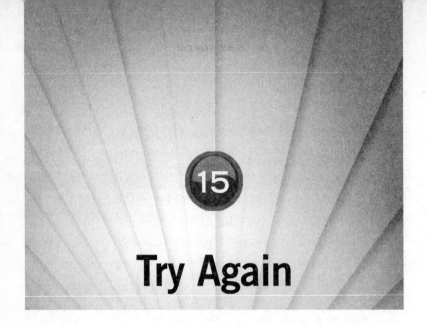

15

Try Again

Astronaut Buzz Aldrin, along with Neil Armstrong, was one of the first two men to ever step foot on the moon. After jumping off the last step of the Apollo 11 lunar module's ladder, Buzz paused to gaze at the panorama. The moon's surface looked like gray ash, pocked with thousands of craters. With no atmosphere on the moon, there was no haze and the sky was crystal clear, so Buzz could easily see a mile and a half away, where the horizon curved into infinity. Above the lunar module, more than a quarter million miles away, a bluish marble of a planet, appearing no bigger than Buzz's thumb, hung suspended in the black, starless sky. It was Buzz and Neil's home—Earth.

"Beautiful view!" Buzz said as much to himself as to Neil.

"Isn't that something?" Neil responded. "Magnificent sight out here."

Buzz gazed in amazement at the majesty of the moon's stark, monochromatic hues and spontaneously said, "Magnificent desolation."

It was a phrase that would take on new meaning for Buzz Aldrin once he returned to earth and hit some serious craters in his own life. After a yearlong, round-the-world tour, in which Buzz and his fellow Apollo 11 astronauts presented chunks of moon rock to presidents, kings, and other leaders as goodwill gestures on behalf of the United States, Buzz returned home, ostensibly to resume "normal life."

That didn't happen. Nothing was normal about Buzz's life anymore. During the year Buzz had been away, the space program had moved on without him. Except as a resource person and a public relations speechmaker, Buzz was no longer needed. Almost overnight, he went from being on top of the world to feeling useless, worthless, and washed up. He had no goals, no projects on which to work, no lofty aspirations. What does a man do for a challenge after he's literally kicked up dust on the moon? He was only thirty-nine years of age, at the top of his game, and one of the first two human beings ever to set foot on another terrestrial body in space. The entire world had watched and listened to him and felt the tension of the almost disastrous landing, and the exhilaration of his dramatic return to earth.

Now, he couldn't find a reason to get out of bed. So he didn't. He passed off his "blues" as fatigue and spent most of the day and evening staring at a television set, getting up only to go to the bathroom, or to get something to eat—or to drink.

Always prone to abusing alcohol, Buzz began to drink more heavily. He became increasingly moody and dismissive of his wife and children, seeking his solace occasionally in another woman, and most frequently in another generous shot of Scotch. Before long, Buzz Aldrin, American hero, plunged into alcoholism and depression. He sought help and spent four weeks in a military psychiatric hospital, then went back to work as though everything was fine. Nothing had changed. His marriage dissolved in an alcohol-induced blur, the depression intensified, and Buzz ignominiously retired from the Air Force.

When Buzz tried to explain his mental and emotional troughs to his family and friends, they looked back at him as if to say, "Depression? What's depression?" People supposedly didn't "get depressed" in Buzz's day, especially soldiers. They just got up and toughed it out. "What's your problem, Buzz? You're a pilot. You are an MIT-educated scientist; for goodness sakes, man, you walked on the *moon*! Surely you can get it together in Los Angeles."

But he couldn't.

Buzz wrote a book, *Return to Earth*, which was made into a television movie starring Cliff Robertson, describing his triumphs and failures, including his bout with what he called "the blue funk," his proclivity for depression. He was one of the first internationally known public figures to admit to a mental/emotional illness, and many of his contemporaries castigated him for doing so, but Buzz continued to raise the specter of mental illness. All the while, he continued to drink a fifth of Scotch or Jack Daniels almost every day. He even served on the board of the National Association for Mental Health (NAMH) and made public appearances on behalf of mental health issues. At the same time, he often fell into funks that lasted for days, in which he refused to get out of bed, sometimes even missing NAMH speaking engagements at which he was the headliner.

He drank his way through another marriage and another divorce within two years. Unemployed, depressed, and drinking ever heavily, Buzz Aldrin, now one of only twelve human beings in the history of mankind to walk on the moon, took a job as a car salesman at a dealership in Beverly Hills. He never sold a single car.

How low does a person need to go before looking up? Of course, that is a difficult question for anyone who has ever battled mental illness, alcoholism, drug addiction, or any other substance abuse. For Buzz, the turning point came when in an inebriated stupor, he broke down the door of a woman he had met at an AA meeting—a woman whom Buzz ironically hoped to help, despite his own alcoholism and depression. When the police cuffed Buzz and took him downtown, his one call was to a friend who would eventually become his sponsor in AA. The friend told him bluntly, "If you want to drink, you are an adult. Go ahead, but don't bother me."

Buzz completed one four-week rehabilitation program after another, all to no avail. Finally, he began attending Alcoholics Anonymous meetings, and got free from the booze—for a while. He earned a number of one-month chips, then three-month chips, and others, only to slip back into drinking. But with the encouragement of some good mentors who understood that relapse was not only possible, but probable, Buzz stopped drinking altogether.

Buzz tells the story: "Finally, in October 1978, I laid down alcohol once and for all. My willingness to do so was not an act of willpower so much as a coming to the end of my own selfishness. I had always been self-centered, and because of my abilities or my intelligence or my fame, people had let me get away with it. When I began to see myself for what I really was, and had a group of fellow travelers who knew me for what I was—and were not impressed—I began to take baby steps toward getting well."[12] Today it has been more than thirty years since Buzz Aldrin has taken a drink, but relapses were part of his life for quite a while.

A Realistic Way to Regard Relapses

Have you known someone who was addicted to some life-challenging behavior, and who got free, only to fall off the wagon, or slip back into using drugs again, overeating, gambling irresponsibly, or some other compulsive behavior?

Our first response is to say, "Oh, how could she? How could he? He was doing so well! She had stopped smoking and had been living free from hoarding for six months, and now she's doing both again! How awful!"

It is awful, but it is also quite normal. Recovery is an ongoing process, so it is not unusual or surprising when someone "falls off the wagon," or gives in to temptation and slips back into previous patterns. Many people struggling with alcoholism, drug addictions, depression, or other mental illnesses begin rehab programs five or ten times before they are able to finally stay clean and sober. The same is true for people trying to overcome weight-loss issues or other compulsive behaviors. That is nothing to be embarrassed about.

My friend, interventionist Dan Cronin, worked with Felipe, a former "debt collector" for the Mafia. Felipe was clean of drugs and alcohol for several years when one morning he called Dan.

"I really messed up," Felipe said, the frustration obvious in his voice.

"What happened?"

"Some guy was giving me a hard time so I popped him!"

Dan recognized the background noise on the line. "Wait a minute," Dan interrupted. "Where are you right now?"

"I'm at the spirituality meeting," Felipe responded.

"You're at the spirituality meeting and you beat up somebody?"

"Well, at least I didn't shoot him!"

That's progress.

So, establish realistic expectations. Those who piously or pompously proclaim that "Failure is not an option" rarely succeed. Failure is *always* an option. It is always possible to slip and fall, or to make wrong choices. But don't despair. If you stumble or flounder, don't give up. Recognize where you went wrong, and get back on the path and start moving forward again. Focus on your victories rather than the times you've slipped up. Falling is always difficult and often embarrassing, even more so when your fall is known in public or you slip in front of the eyes of the friends or family who have been trying to help you. Wallowing in disappointment only makes it feel worse.

Slips and falls happen, but don't allow them to keep you down and to define the rest of your life. Get up and get back on track.

What's the Difference Between a Lapse and Relapse?

A "lapse" is a temporary slipup, and it may take various forms. Perhaps after being free from alcohol for two years, you take a drink at a party, or worse yet, you get drunk. Or you stop taking medications that help keep your system on keel. Or after getting clean from drugs, you take a hit of cocaine. Or you go out for dinner at a great Italian restaurant and pig out on pasta.

These isolated, short-term slipups are lapses, and they are a normal part of a long-term renewal of your mindset. The key is: When a lapse happens, you recognize it as an aberration. That is no longer the person you are. You are different; you have a new mindset now, and you can use the lapse as an opportunity to learn.

Unfortunately, many people who slip up also slip backward, into their former mindsets; they see themselves as a failure, a total idiot for falling off the wagon. If that lapse isn't turned into a learning opportunity, Jeff might say, "Aw, what's the use. I've already had one drink. I might as well have a few more." Or Samantha might give up in despair, thinking, "I'm never going to keep my weight in check. I enjoy food too much. That pasta tasted so good at dinner. I've already blown my eating plan. I might as well have some cake and ice cream, too."

Even that would not be the end of the world if Jeff and Samantha realized the error of those attitudes and rebounded back to their normal maintenance program. It is only when you allow a lapse to become long-term that it becomes a *relapse*, which may last a few weeks or months, or may send you reeling into old negative thought patterns, habits, and attitudes that will lead you back to drinking, using drugs, overeating, or other actions and activities from which you had been freed.

While I don't agree with the notion that "once an alcoholic, always an alcoholic," we should avoid giving the impression that breaking a habit is an irrevocable decision. Truth is, most people who eventually get free and stay free have numerous lapses and relapses. That's why we need to recognize and understand that lapses and relapses are *normal*. Beyond that, if we hope to maintain a life we love free of addictions and substance abuses, we need to *prepare* for relapses, and have a good idea of how we will respond when they happen. That doesn't mean we condone the slipups or encourage them. But it is critical that we expect lapses and relapses in our lives or that of someone we are trying to help, and are not so discouraged when they occur that we give up in despair of ever getting free.

You Don't Have to Start Over

Having a lapse or even a relapse does not mean you must go back to square one and start all over again. It simply means you need to acknowledge the destructive actions and get back on the right path.

Sometimes a person may experience several relapses before he or she learns how to handle the cravings that still come at the most vulnerable moments, but don't give up. Keep renewing your mindset and keep pressing forward toward the life you want to live.

In any transformation, it is important that you expect that lapses and relapses will occur. That is not negative thinking; it is establishing realistic expectations. When lapses or relapses happen, simply learn what you can from the experience regarding why it happened, then pick right up where you were, moving forward from that point rather than starting over from the beginning.

If you are working through a lapse or helping someone else do so, the essential ingredient to keep in mind is: HOPE, believable hope that change is possible, that change is slowly but surely occurring and that lapses and relapses will eventually become less frequent, and eventually nonexistent.

Using Scars to Help Save Others

I was standing in the driveway of one of our West Coast treatment centers when Dallas Taylor pulled in to attend a luncheon tour. I welcomed him to our facility, and as soon as I began chatting with him, I recognized his passion to help families who were dealing with the effects of alcoholism and addiction. The National Council on Alcoholism estimates that every alcoholic in the United States directly affects at least four other people, usually family members or friends. Because of embarrassment or guilt, family members sometimes try to cover the destructive behavior of the alcoholic or addict or make excuses if the addiction becomes known. Spouses and children will often adjust their whole lives around the addicted person, frequently going through psychological changes themselves in their efforts to protect the addicted family member. As the addicted person becomes more immersed in his or her alcoholism, the family members become more involved as well—and not always in positive ways. In the process, they not only enable the addiction to continue, but the family members often become sick themselves.

Dallas Taylor had lived with the effects of alcoholism and drugs in his own life and family. He knew all too well the devastating toll that substance abuse takes upon those close to an addict or alcoholic.

His mom died when Dallas was thirteen, and his father, a famous stunt pilot, was killed in an air show accident when Dallas was sixteen. Dallas developed an intense insecurity and self-loathing, which he attempted to hide beneath a haze of drugs and alcohol as he began an elusive quest for love and acceptance. Dallas found a sense of acceptance through music, playing in bars as a thirteen-year-old—bars he couldn't get into on his own, so his mother accompanied him. At seventeen years of age, Dallas played drums for Clear Light, a rock band signed to the same manager as the Doors. Through that, Dallas met and worked with John Sebastian, formerly of the Lovin' Spoonful, and eventually became friends with Crosby, Stills, and Nash. Dallas played with the band on their first self-titled, hit album. Neil Young later joined the band as well.

During Dallas's musical career, he traveled the world and played drums on albums that sold multiple millions of copies. He became known as one of the best drummers in the world. Unfortunately, he also got heavily into cocaine and eventually addicted to heroin. He took his first hit of cocaine during a recording session. Dallas recalls, "I reluctantly snorted a little bit of white powder, and immediately my throat closed up and for a few moments, I couldn't breathe. And then I asked for some more."

He became friends and hung out with Jimi Hendrix, Janis Joplin, Jim Morrison, and other superstars—all who died drug-related deaths in their mid-twenties. As a member of the supergroup CSN&Y, jetting around the world in their own Boeing 707 from one concert venue to another, Dallas discovered an endless supply of drugs. Dallas's own addictions to cocaine led to heavy drinking, combined with pills, as he desperately tried to maintain his buzz. Music moved from the most important thing in his life to becoming simply a means of getting more drugs. His career crashed and burned within a few years. When it did, Dallas no longer wanted to live.

Dallas sought help to kick the heroin at a treatment center in Phoenix, but he had no intention of giving up his drinking. Within a short time, Dallas was kicked out of the treatment center due to his unwillingness to comply with the program.

Back in Los Angeles, he attempted suicide, stabbing himself with a butcher knife. But he was too weak even to kill himself. He was taken to a hospital, then upon his release was taken to a drug rehabilitation center.

When Dallas woke up in the treatment center, he was considered the person least likely to survive, much less succeed. Yet because he had such a sense of entitlement left over from being a rock star, he balked when the treatment center would not give him a room with his own television. "What am I going to do here all day?" he asked belligerently. Fortunately, his counselor was a former biker chick who had seen Dallas's kind too many times. She quickly informed him that he had a distorted sense of himself.

The first thing the staff at the treatment center did was to help Dallas go through detoxification, allowing the drugs and alcohol to work their way out of his system, then replacing medications only as needed. It was not a pretty sight. Dallas crouched in a corner like an animal and lashed out verbally and sometimes physically at anyone who came near him. But when he made it through twenty-four hours without drinking or using drugs, suddenly he had hope that he might be able to get clean. That didn't mean it was easy. He was in detox for more than a month.

He nearly got tossed from that treatment center as well, but the director came to his defense. Dallas stayed. He finally got sober, ten years after becoming addicted, although that would not prevent him from needing a liver transplant and a kidney transplant five years later. His liver looked literally like a piece of volcanic lava, as a result of the alcohol and drugs. Nevertheless, Dallas never looked back. He maintained his sobriety.

When Dallas left the treatment center, his first instinct was to get back in the music business, but his counselor told him, "No, you need to get a job, a humble job." The last job Dallas had other than his music career was when he was ten years old, washing cars. But Dallas was willing to do anything necessary to maintain the new life he had discovered, so he considered the counselor's options.

"You have two choices," the counselor told him. "We can help you get a job at Pizza Hut, or we can help you get on as a tech at the Adolescent Recovery Unit, where you can work with young addicted kids." Dallas had no idea what working at the recovery unit involved, but he feared that if he worked at Pizza Hut, somebody might recognize him, and that would be too shameful. So he chose the job doing "grunt work" for the kids.

Dallas fell in love with working with alcoholic and addicted kids and their families. He had a gift for relating to the young people, many of whom were between the ages of thirteen and eighteen. Being a member of a world-famous band gave him an entrée to the young kids, and they were willing to listen to him when he told them his story of how drugs and alcohol had robbed and ruined him.

Soon, his bosses recognized that Dallas could be of more help in counseling sessions than he could by washing the van, and they began to train him in intervention methods. While there, Dallas was trained by Dave Lewis, John Bradshaw, Kip Flock, and Paul Tobias, some of the early greats in the recovery field.

Dallas eventually came to work for us as a consultant and became a tremendous asset in improving our family program. He worked with us as an outside contractor for more than five years.

Dallas worked with numerous famous or wealthy Hollywood stars or musicians. "What are you doing here?" Dallas was asked often. "Why aren't you out enjoying your yacht?"

He pointed to the scars on his arm. "That's where all my money went," he responded. The clients nodded in understanding.

One of the high-profile clients with whom Dallas worked was Robert Downey Jr., a talented actor who because of his addictions could not maintain his work. Acting was in his blood, since his father and mother were both in the business, but drugs and alcohol were also in his blood, since Robert's father was a heavy user. By 1996, Robert was a Hollywood box-office star, but his own demons were more frightening than any horror movie. Between 1996 and 2001, Robert went through several drug treatment programs, but with no apparent change. He was arrested repeatedly on drug-related charges, including possession of cocaine, heroin, and marijuana, and even did a stint in California State Prison in 2000. Robert appeared on the hit television show *Ally McBeal*, but was fired after more drug-related arrests. His life was out of control, and his every attempt to manage it proved futile. He once told a judge, "It's like I've got a shotgun in my mouth with my finger on the trigger, and I like the taste of the gun metal."

Dallas could relate to Robert, and perhaps more importantly, Robert could relate to Dallas, who had been at the top of the music world, but had plummeted to the pits of despair because of his addictions.

Dallas began with Robert simply by telling him his story and Robert understood it all too well. He made great progress, but then Robert relapsed several more times before finally getting clean. His career rebounded, and in recent years, Robert Downey Jr. has become box-office gold once again with his roles in *Sherlock Holmes*, *The Avengers*, and other hit movies.

In November 2004, Robert shared his story of substance abuse, arrests, rehabs, and relapses with Oprah Winfrey on her television show. Clean and sober, Robert encouraged others to seek help. "When someone says, 'I really wonder if maybe I should go to rehab?' Well, ah, you're a wreck, you just lost your job, and your wife left you. You might want to give it a shot." Regarding the most difficult aspect of getting clean, Robert replied, "It's not that difficult to overcome these seemingly ghastly problems. . . . What's hard is to decide to actually do it."

Now more than twenty-eight years clean and sober, somewhere Dallas Taylor was smiling . . . . and so was I. Whether it is an addicted Hollywood superstar or a homeless alcoholic living under a bridge, that sort of transformation is what our lives are all about.

You're Not Alone

Certainly you can empathize with those feelings of despair that come with lapses. "I'm never going to get free of this stuff!" or "What's wrong with me? Why can't I just say no to those fattening foods?"

Understand and acknowledge that others who are working on transforming their lives also experience lapses; you are not alone or unusual, and just as others have regained their footing after a slip or a fall, you can, too. You are not a weakling, you just need help. And we are here to help you. Our goal is your success, so we will continue to bolster you with believable hope, while guarding your pride and dignity.

> Go confidently in the direction of your dreams. Live the life you have imagined.
>
> —*Henry David Thoreau*

Triggers to Relapse

What are some common reasons people relapse?

If a person is in recovery, any lifestyle change, such as a job loss or a family conflict, can lead to a relapse. Stress, too, is a major cause of relapses. I understand this all too well, because I am a food addict. I no longer drink alcohol or take any sort of euphoric drugs, but I love to eat! And it is a totally acceptable addiction, as far as other people are concerned. For many people, food is one of the most difficult addictions with which to deal. After all, we don't have to do drugs or drink alcohol, but we do need to eat.

For me, food is a euphoric stress-reliever. When my life gets stressed for one reason or another, as it often does, I am tempted to turn to tasty comfort foods such as cakes, pies, and ice cream. I know better; I am fully aware that these foods are not good for me, yet I sometimes succumb to the temptation to eat them. I recognize that this is a lifetime struggle. I have to continually renew my mindset to make healthy choices. If I blow it once in a while, that is one thing, but to continue down that path is not a plan for me. Besides my personal integrity and desires, I own Fit-RX, a weight-loss company, and I'm an owner in SEALFIT. I cannot afford to let myself be a slacker.

I was working out with Brent, a client at Fit-RX who had weighed more than 340 pounds when he came to us. He did well for a while, and dropped more than eighty pounds, but then he hit the wall, and couldn't make further progress. Worse yet, he actually put on some weight. He was doing a vigorous workout, so I knew that he had to be eating incorrectly. Rather than castigating him for eating poorly, I told him about my own recent experience. "I just haven't been eating right," I confided to Brent. "I've been overeating for the past six months. I know it is stress related. I'm still working out, but I've not been eating right and I've put on about fifteen pounds, so I'm going to adjust my eating habits and get it off." I was hoping that by telling Brent about my own relapse, he would recognize the reasons for his.

He didn't. So I tried a more overt method.

"I have a question for you, Brent. You work out here five days a week, but you are still overweight. We're burning about seven hundred calories every workout, so it must be something else."

"I know you're right, Michael," he said. "I've been eating terribly."

"I'm telling you my story, because you aren't making progress, and you probably know why. You're going backwards."

"Yes, I do. At night, I eat too much, I overindulge, and eat a lot of wrong things."

"Okay, I'll make you a deal," I said. "Let's make it a contest to see who can lose the most weight before the end of the year. Are you in?"

"You're on."

"Alright, I want you to write down everything you eat or drink for the next thirty days. And be honest. If you eat some chocolate cake, write it down. Don't lie. It's not about showing me. You have to be honest with yourself. Once we establish a baseline, and determine how many calories you are taking in compared to your metabolism and the calories we are burning in our workouts, we can figure out where you are slipping up."

Brent took the challenge and got back on track. That's the key.

Remember, relapse can occur with weight loss, mental illness, or addictions. The causes are basically the same. And the solutions are the same, too. Don't give up, but when you slip up, get back up and get moving forward again!

Subtle Warning Signs

Just as reflective signs warn a driver speeding down Pacific Highway 1 that there are dangerous curves and sharp cliffs ahead, certain warning signs will alert you that you may be nearing the precipice of a relapse cliff. Changes in attitude, changes in behavior, losing interest in the recovery plan, or taking over-the-counter medications without checking with a physician are all subtle warning signs that something is awry. In the same way, skipping doses of prescribed medications, dishonest dealings, or missing work, school, or other commitments should be red flags that we are nearing a dangerous area.

Some subtle warning signs could include the following statements or thoughts:

"I'm just keeping that candy on the coffee table for friends who might drop by."

"I'm not going anywhere; I don't need to wash or take a shower today."

"I don't need therapy anymore. I can handle my problems on my own."

"I wanted to go dancing so I went out to a club where I used to go. I saw some people drinking and doing drugs, but it didn't bother me."

Certainly, some of these statements might be absolutely true. On the other hand, they may be subtle rationalizations, which can lead to trouble. When we first see these negative things showing up, that is the time to begin asking questions and exploring the reasons for the aberrant behaviors. You don't have to wait for a lapse or relapse before seeking help. Moreover, don't disregard help from family members.

Internal changes to consider might include negative thoughts and emotions. Clearly, thoughts and emotions are linked, so if one changes, the other is sure to follow. External changes might involve other people, places, and activities having a negative affect. Again, these may be linked; change one and the other will change. But if the subtle signs can be spotted early enough, many relapses can be prevented.

Obvious Warning Signs

The obvious warning signs are usually more easily detected but unfortunately, these also tend to lead to high-risk situations. When you hear yourself or someone else glorifying substance use or rationalizing the use of another substance, beware. Something is amiss. Similarly, profound mood shifts for no apparent reason can indicate that a relapse is a real possibility. Not sleeping—or the opposite, not wanting to get out of bed all day—or staying out walking the streets at night, changes in eating habits, or ignoring your personal responsibilities are major red flags. Discontinuing treatment or attendance at self-help support groups, and thoughts of harming oneself are also burning flares signaling that a relapse could be in the making.

Some obvious warning signs could include statements or thoughts such as the following:

"I've lost my will to live. Nobody cares whether I live or die, so why should I?"

"I'm going to stop by the old neighborhood and see if any of my friends are still around. I haven't seen them in ages, and it would be great to reconnect."

"I haven't slept for a couple of days, and I'm still not tired. I'm wired and ready for some action."

"I think somebody is out to get me. That's why I'm keeping the blinds closed and my doors locked."

These signs often come in the form of triggers—activities, events, or people that tend to activate symptoms in a person who is recovering from addictions or compulsive behaviors. Oftentimes, these triggers fall into all-too-familiar patterns, usually involving a series of poor decisions, as a person sets himself or herself up for failure.

For instance, Erin was doing well in her recovery plan, beating back her alcoholism for more than a year, but then she got laid off at her job and broke up with her boyfriend in the same week. She felt awful about herself—inept, rejected, and unwanted. When she drove by a neighborhood bar where she and her friends formerly hung out, she literally began perspiring. Her heart began beating more rapidly, and she could feel herself fidgeting in the driver's seat. She made it past the bar, but then she stopped at the nearest ATM machine to get some money. She decided to stop back by the bar "just to grab a sandwich," and see if any of her former drinking buddies were there.

I'm not going to drink, she told herself repeatedly. *I just want to see if any of my friends are around.*

Of course, they were. And naturally, Erin's friends were drinking when she walked into the establishment. Erin joined them at their table, and her friends commiserated with her over the lost job and boyfriend. Before long, Erin was feeling even more sorry for herself, and her anxiety level was increasing with each round of fresh drinks. "Why bother?" she rationalized. "I've been trying so hard to be good, and where has it gotten me? One drink won't hurt, and it might calm me down."

Unfortunately, that one drink led to another . . . and another . . . and another, until Erin was heading for a full-scale relapse.

All along the way to Erin's relapse, there were obvious triggers that she recognized, and could have taken as warning signs to take some proactive actions to avoid the relapse. For instance, after the emotional setbacks of losing her job and boyfriend in the same week, she could have called a sober friend, a fellow church member, or family member and let that support person know that she was feeling vulnerable, that she needed to surround herself with clean and sober people right now.

Even driving by the bar could have raised a red flag to her. Rather than stopping in that neighborhood, she could have driven straight to a sober friend's place. Once she stopped, and especially when she obtained some cash, she was opening the door to temptation. Even then, instead of going into the bar to eat, she could have given herself some healthy treat or reward, saying, "I'm worth it. I'm going to go see that movie I've wanted to see," or "I am going to eat at that classy new restaurant tonight." Taking a walk, engaging in some physical activity that helps blow off stress would have been a good choice, too.

Surrounding herself with her former friends, all of whom were drinking, was another point where rather than wallowing in negative comments and thoughts, Erin could have seen the warning signs. She might have reminded herself, *I can get through this without drinking. I am going to dwell on good thoughts, seeing myself as the sober person I want to be.* A quick hello to her friends, and a hasty exit, may have saved her from the relapse.

When you recognize the triggers—and they may be different for various people—take immediate steps to seek support. Obviously, the earlier you recognize the warning signs, the sooner you can take the positive steps to avoid trouble. And the better you will feel about yourself for having overcome a temptation. This is a major key to recovery—learning to respond to the warning signs so that you can stop relapses before they happen.

Unpredictable Warning Signs

Sometimes relapses can be triggered by familiar people, places, or activities that were once a part of your past destructive behaviors. Sarah admitted, "It was stressful going back home for the holidays, so I went out with some friends to a party and ended up drinking again."

Oftentimes, merely being in a negative environment—especially an environment you formerly frequented—can trigger cravings even though you are clean and taking care of yourself. Intense desires can sometimes pop up and seemingly appear out of the blue. Rich admitted, "I ran in to an old friend downtown, and he offered me some crack. It was too easy, so I took it. Then I went back and bought some more."

Unpredictable triggers are difficult to prevent. You may simply be going about your life when you see or hear something that sends your mind down a wrong path. For instance, a former hoarder may be walking through a shopping mall, when she is suddenly overwhelmed with the desire to go on an impulsive shopping spree, purchasing things she neither needs nor can afford.

A person dealing with a gambling addiction may be watching a football game on television when struck by an intense desire to bet on the game. Similarly, beer commercials and food advertisements can derail an alcoholic or a person battling with weight issues. Seeing an old photograph of a former lover may send reeling a person dealing with sex addiction. These individuals may have been "doing all the right things," when that sudden, seemingly irresistible urge is stimulated by normal, everyday activities.

But that is precisely why lasting transformation requires the mindset component. It is impossible to totally prevent temptation, but you can learn how to control your responses and take positive actions that will keep you on track.

In most situations, taking immediate protective steps to change the activity or thought process can usually prevent relapse—in the cases mentioned above, the hoarder could quickly exit the mall, the gambler, alcoholic, or food addict could change channels to something that takes his or her mind in a healthier direction. The temptation toward inappropriate sexual activity might be overcome simply by getting rid of that tempting photograph. These steps aren't rocket science. But they take enormous effort, willpower, and most of all, a believable hope that the avoidance of the triggers can be accomplished and is worth it.

Turn Your Nights and Weekends into Restorative Times

It's no secret that long, lonely nights or leisurely weekends can be conducive to relapses. If you are accustomed to going out socializing at night, fine; choose a place where people are engaging in positive activities, rather than indulging in the behavior you are overcoming. You may love to dance, yet so many places that cater to the dance crowd also attract a drinking crowd, and often a drug crowd. But with a little effort, you can find "nonalcoholic" dances sponsored by Alcoholics Anonymous groups, Dual Recovery Anonymous groups, church social groups, and others. It is unwise to put yourself in an environment where other people are engaging in the very activities that you know are counterproductive in your life.

If you are overcoming weight issues, don't allow yourself to come home from work and flop onto the couch in front of the television all night or weekend. Go for walks, ride a bike, join a volleyball team or a golf league, start a hobby—something, anything that will get you out of the house and into an activity that not only helps lower stress levels, but allows you to interact with other people overcoming similar issues.

Moreover, if you are trying to lose weight, but you constantly allow yourself to be around people who are overeaters, you are going to have much more difficulty maintaining a healthy diet. You need to be around people who are supportive of your efforts to lose weight. Some people may support the idea of you dropping some pounds, but they continue to eat poorly in your presence. That isn't helpful to you.

Understand, these are not bad people, but the facilitators and enablers around you can bring you down because of their own issues or the buttons they push on you by offering you opportunities to fudge on your transformation process.

Cindy's mom chides her daughter about her weight all the time. "You're never going to find anyone to marry if you don't lose twenty pounds," she says. At the same time, Cindy's mom eats poorly herself and out of love for her daughter keeps facilitating her backsliding. "Have a piece of pie and a bit of this new flavor of ice cream," she'll say.

"Mom, I'm on a diet," Cindy will remind her mother.

"Oh, I know, but one little piece of pie isn't going to hurt you."

Oh, yes it will. Fat cells never go away. They can be reduced and controlled, but if you feed them ice cream and cake, they will expand all over again, taking you right back where you don't want to be.

The same is true with people who do drugs and alcohol. "You need to quit," friends or family members may say. But when you finally quit, they continue drinking around you or continue doing drugs in your presence. Granted, you may be the one who has the problem, but the people around you have some responsibility to help you by not offering constant temptations to drag you back into the lifestyle you are trying to leave. Choose to avoid situations in which you are vulnerable to temptations, and instead, find people and places where you can set yourself up for success.

Weekends can be particularly conducive to discouragement if you are alone. Go to a meeting, or attend a service at a church or synagogue. Attend a lecture or an uplifting movie or concert. Just don't allow yourself to remain inactive and invite opportunities to relapse.

Tempting Faces

We tend to think that temptation will come dressed as something evil, but often the most difficult times are being around family or friends who are still indulging in the very substances or activities you are overcoming. You won't be able to avoid all such situations, so you have to prepare a plan in advance for how you will deal with them. Most tempting situations can be diffused if you have already established in your mind that you will take a different tack.

Say that you go home for a family birthday party and everyone is overeating or drinking alcohol, and you are conquering weight issues or alcoholism. Plan in advance how you will deal with the kindness of your friends and family. In most cases, they are not trying to sabotage your efforts; they just don't understand that you cannot afford a single step backward.

When someone offers you food, drugs, alcohol, or another substance you are trying to avoid, you needn't respond in some belligerent or harsh manner. Simply say, "No thanks, but I would love to have a glass of water" (or a soft drink, or some other healthy alternative). By doing so, you are accepting the kind gesture while offering an alternative that fits with your recovery plan. But remember, it is always wise for you to have some alternatives in mind before you attend such events or find yourself in situations where you are around people whose activities may be counterproductive for you. Don't depend on anyone else to make these suggestions. You must come up with them.

Dealing with Your Cravings

Sometimes the temptations don't come from others, but the urge to return to your former patterns pops up in your own mind or body. You may be driving down the highway on a beautiful day, and suddenly your mind turns to thoughts of drinking or using drugs. Oftentimes, people who are in the process of overcoming addictions find themselves having recurring dreams of drinking or doing drugs. These cravings are normal—especially during the first few years of staying clean—and are often triggered by certain people, places, or previous experiences that linger in your mind. The temptations will usually pass relatively quickly if you can blink your eyes, choose to dwell on positive thoughts, and change your present environment or activity. Your new mindset will help you to get through those tough times, and with each victory, you will emerge stronger and more confident.

Some simple keys can help you (or the person you are trying to help) overcome your own cravings:

First and foremost, get away from any tempting situations. Don't hang around negative-minded people who might bring you down. Instead, take steps to put yourself in an environment where people will encourage you to maintain your recovery.

Second, contact someone who is supportive of your recovery, not just someone who loves you. Family and close friends may not always be your best resources, since they are often in denial, or perhaps their advice may not be wise regarding the overcoming process you have chosen. My contact information is in the back of this book; feel free to contact us day or night.

Third, react in the opposite spirit. Just about the time you don't want to go to an AA meeting or a church service or a DRA group meeting, that is probably the best time for you to go. When you want to pig out on pasta or ice cream, that's a good time for a walk around the neighborhood. If you are tempted to pull the covers over your face rather than facing the day, that is when you want to get up and do some exercises. Generally, when you feel yourself leaning toward unhealthy behavior, that is the time to depend on your new mindset to help you do the opposite. You will not only feel better physically, but you will feel good about yourself emotionally.

Fourth, keep your progress in mind. Remember where you came from and be grateful that you don't live there anymore; you are changed, transformed, and in many ways, not that same person who lived with addictions or compulsive behaviors. It is good to appreciate where you were, but don't dwell there; focus on the person you believe you are becoming.

Fifth, pray. Many people find incredible strength to overcome their past addictions by reaching out and asking for help. When I was coming off alcohol and drugs, I used to pray the Serenity Prayer five times in succession, at least four times a day. Most people know the first stanza of the famous prayer. The prayer has been altered slightly over the years, but Reinhold Niebuhr's prayer actually consists of even more profound thoughts:

> *God grant me the serenity to accept the things I cannot change;*
> *Courage to change the things I can; and wisdom to know the difference.*
> *Living one day at a time;*
> *Enjoying one moment at a time;*
> *Accepting hardships as the pathway to peace;*
> *Taking, as He did, this sinful world*
> *As it is, not as I would have it;*
> *Trusting that He will make all things right*
> *If I surrender to His Will;*
> *That I may be reasonably happy in this life*
> *And supremely happy with Him*
> *Forever in the next.*
> *Amen.*

I found incredible peace and confidence by praying the Serenity Prayer, and I still pray it to this day. Years ago, my grandmother made me a beautiful quilt bearing the Serenity Prayer, and I keep it prominently displayed in my office. I never want to forget where the real power comes from.

However you choose to pray, call out to your Higher Power and that spiritual connection will give you confidence, too. Ask God to help you, and to give you the power to stay on the right path.

Dealing with mental illness relapse is similar to this as well. Depression may lead a person to start drinking or using drugs again in hopes of feeling better, or the opposite can occur. He or she may use drugs or drink and then become depressed as a result. Often, it is difficult to tell which came first, the depression or the relapse. Regardless, they will both need to be addressed.

Not surprisingly, people frequently offer irrational reasons for their relapses.

Renee said, "I was feeling better, so I thought I could stop taking my medications."

Bryan said, "When my friend offered me a beer, I took it. I just didn't know how to say no."

"I don't know why you think I've been using again," Tim told his counselor. "There must be some mistake."

"I'm really confused," Tim's counselor responded without accusing him of lying. "You reported that you haven't used, yet your drug screen was positive."

"Yeah, well, I guess I did use a little bit," Tim acknowledged.

"Alright. Thanks for telling me," the counselor replied. "Let's establish some new goals and move on from here."

How Much Do You Want It?

Real recovery takes time and work. How committed are you to your new way of life? One of the questions I ask an individual who claims to want a transformation in his or her life is, "Are you willing to spend three hours every day working on your recovery?"

Most people who are serious about improving their lives are willing to put forth the effort because they recognize the importance of making a lifestyle change. When I was using drugs, I used to walk five miles in the rain or snow to get a fix. Many addicts and alcoholics spend twelve hours a day on their negative behavior, so to ask a person to commit three hours a day to positive change is not an unreasonable request. I ask, "Can you give me three hours a day to achieve a positive change in your life?"

I also ask, "Will you write down the amount of time you spend on your plan of action, working on your daily change?"

I've never met anyone who consistently puts in three hours a day working on his or her recovery who regularly relapses. They just don't. Instead, they continue to move forward. Oh, sure, occasionally, someone will slip and fall, but he or she gets right back up again, learns from the mistake, and moves forward in his or her life.

How to Limit Relapses

If you want to limit relapses, here's what I suggest: Start each day by spending ten to twenty minutes in meditation with God. Pray, talk to God, think on good things. Read some positive material that reinforces your lifestyle change. Get some exercise; walk, run, swim, ride a bike, do something to move your body. Go to a meeting where you will be encouraged. Attend a church function. Put yourself in a position to meet positive-minded people. And do these kinds of things for three hours a day, every day.

Just Don't Quit!

Remember, recovery and lifestyle change are ongoing processes. Don't beat yourself up if you get off track occasionally. Recall my grandmother's words: "How you respond to the setbacks will define you."

If you are striving to lose weight, but you have a bad day and eat all sorts of junk food, how do you respond? If you fall off the wagon, what are you going to do to get back on?

I tell clients to *expect* to slip once in a while. You may eat something you shouldn't. You might fail to exercise for a few days. Just don't quit. Recognize your mistake as quickly as possible. Then get back on track and move forward again.

Many people give up when they relapse. "Forget it. I knew I could never stay clean. I knew that I couldn't keep up this fitness program."

But the secret to a better future is: If you slip, learn from the experience. Determine what led to this situation and then avoid those triggers in the future.

We all need help at something. If you don't have the skills or the wherewithal, find someone who can help you. If your goal is to lose weight, or to get off drugs or alcohol, who can you hire to help you? Where can you go to find the sort of help that will work? Contact American Addiction Centers (contact information in back of book), and we will help you.

Maintaining your new life and managing your feelings and emotional responses to drugs, alcohol, food, or other temptations are ongoing processes. Your emotions can be adversely affected by all sorts of things in life—everything from an upsetting phone call or a negative response on your social media account, to a tragedy in your family. How you respond makes all the difference. Unmanaged emotional responses can lead to all sorts of unhealthy habits.

You may need to learn how to call a HALT—noting that many problems result from being *hungry, angry, lonely,* or *tired*—thus, the acronym used by many twelve-step programs: HALT. These four feelings, if left unmanaged, can lead to relapsing with alcohol, drugs, food, cigarettes, or other life-controlling issues.

By identifying the events that trigger your emotions, you can focus on better ways of reacting. Concentrate on the rewards of managing those triggers, reminding yourself of the better health, improved self-esteem, increased energy, and freedom that you will enjoy as a result of overcoming your guilty pleasures. As much as possible, keep your thoughts on the healthy lifestyle you want, rather than the destructive behavior you want to avoid.

Have you ever tried to walk on railroad tracks? No, not the rails at Grand Central Station, but have you ever tried to walk the tracks out in the country, where the trains seldom if ever run anymore?

Kids used to do it all the time when I was growing up. I learned an important lesson walking those tracks: if you look down at your feet as you are trying to move forward, inevitably you will fall off. But if you keep your head up and your eyes straight ahead, you can go a long way before slipping, stumbling, or falling down.

The same is true in transformation. You may slip occasionally, but don't despair. Pick up where you left off, and get back on the track. You *can* make it! And we will be right there with you to help you, to hold your hand when necessary, to help you keep your balance, and to encourage you to get back on track when you fall. Remind yourself, "I am not alone; there are people who want to help me through this." And keep that believable hope in mind: "My future is bright as long as I keep working on my transformation."

All Things Are Possible to Him Who Believes

When Jesus encountered a boy who was apparently demonized to the point of suffering convulsions, writhing on the ground, and foaming at the mouth, He asked how long the boy had been enduring these conditions. The boy's father responded that the boy had suffered this way since childhood, and asked, "If you can do anything, have compassion on us and help us."

Jesus responded with a statement that has become known throughout generations. He said, "If you can believe, all things are possible to him who believes."[13] Jose Orozco is living proof of that statement. Jose would not allow adversity of any sort—especially a negative mindset—to keep him down. Born in Cuba in 1968, almost ten years after Fidel Castro's oppressive communist government came to power, Jose discovered early on that the only way he could prosper under that system was to excel academically. He did, his youthful brilliance during Cuba's "Golden Age of Education" catching the attention of party leaders, who sent Jose to the Soviet Union (Russia) to further his education and return to Cuba as an engineer.

As one of Cuba's academic elite, Jose spent six years in Russia studying civil engineering, and received his degrees in structural geology and hydro-geology. The day he returned to Havana, as he stepped out of the plane, the restrictive stagnancy of the Castro government smacked him right in the face. It was as though time had stood still and the country had not progressed. Jose grabbed his head, and thought, *What have I done in returning here? I should have defected when our plane landed in Canada.* Everywhere he looked, the buildings looked old and run down. The people's faces bore hopeless expressions.

But Jose wanted to return to his family, and to contribute to society and help improve his country. He was assigned a job and began his career. He quickly discovered, however, that because of the government's authoritarian rule, he was facing an impossible situation. He was managed by people who did not have nearly the skills or intellect as his, but they were high-ranking party members. As a top-notch, highly educated engineer, Jose earned 148 Cuban pesos a month, which equated to less than one U.S. dollar per month.

Every day was a struggle for survival. People stood in line for everything from trying to get food to getting on a bus. Jose realized that he had received a tremendous education, yet he had little potential because there were no resources available except to those in the upper echelons of the Communist party, and no opportunities to explore his professional life, get married, and provide for a family.

At work, Jose noticed an engineer next to him with several doctoral degrees in engineering, who had been working in the system for twenty years and written numerous professional papers, yet he had no home of his own; he still lived with his parents, even though he was married. He rode to work on a bicycle, and had no opportunity to get ahead in life, even though he was well educated.

Twenty-six-year-old Jose saw his future in his coworker. He, too, had great potential, but no opportunity and no freedom to pursue the life he dreamed about establishing.

I need to get out of here, Jose realized, and he began plotting his escape. It was illegal for anyone to leave the country without the government's permission—a ten-year prison sentence was not uncommon for anyone caught trying to leave the country—so the only way people could escape was to risk their lives in some form of makeshift boat or raft and hope to make the treacherous trip across the Caribbean between Cuba and the United States.

Securing a seaworthy boat was a challenge. It wasn't as though Jose could go to the local dealership and purchase a boat. There were no dealerships, no boats available, and no money to buy a boat even if one could be found. Jose secretly moved around the country and found used materials that he and some friends could weld together as a seaworthy vessel. Working under the cover of darkness, they built a precarious boat made from metal sheeting they cut apart from scrapped irrigation pipe. They secured a two-piston motor that somebody had been using to pump water to irrigate crops.

Originally, fourteen other people planned to leave with Jose. But by the time they were ready to escape, a hurricane blew up over the Caribbean, so only seven men and one woman with a small child dared to risk putting out to sea under such turbulent conditions. In a pelting rain, at about two o'clock in the morning on September 12, 1994, they furtively put their craft into a river and hopped aboard, hoping they could reach the open ocean and head north before being detected. They took no clothing other than what they wore, and had no food but a sack of sugar and a fifty-gallon tank of water.

Out on the open sea, they faced the full fury of the hurricane, the sound of the wind like that of a roaring lion in the jungle. Their tiny boat was tossed about on waves as high as a building, and they lost their bearings for several days. The escapees had no idea where they were heading, but they dared not turn back. Finally after four days in the inclement weather, a fishing boat spotted the refugees' boat floundering in the sea. The fishing boat contacted the U.S. Coast Guard, which picked up Jose and his friends and transferred them to a U.S. Navy destroyer that took the refugees, not to Miami, but back to Cuba, to Guantanamo Bay military base.

Already 35,000 Cubans had been rescued trying to reach America and they were all housed at Guantanamo. When Jose and his friends arrived at Gitmo, it was already overcrowded, so when the military asked for volunteers to go to Panama, Jose volunteered. After four months in Panama, Jose was returned to Guantanamo again.

Existence at Gitmo for the refugees was difficult. Living in tents housing twelve cots each, with no toilets or running water, the refugees received military MREs, meals ready to eat, and a military water truck came around each morning so they could fill buckets for their daily needs. Many of the refugees simply sat around smoking cigarettes all day, rolling dice, and waiting for something to happen.

Not Jose. When Jose arrived at Gitmo, he could speak no English, but each day, he listened to soldiers giving instructions in English. One of the soldiers gave Jose an elementary school history book, another gave him a dictionary, and Jose literally taught himself rudimentary English within five months. He learned the language so well that when the United Way arrived and began trying to help the refugees make the transition to freedom, they tapped Jose as a translator and a teacher. Eventually, he volunteered as a translator for the doctors working in the camp's naval hospital emergency room. His positive attitude and willingness to work paid off big-time.

When Jose was finally transferred from the camp after more than a year, the commander of the Navy hospital gave him a glowing letter of recommendation. Jose was taken to Massachusetts, where he began the search for a job as an engineer.

Jose used his recommendation letter to his advantage and was hired to teach in English as a Second Language programs. He applied to a community college and was given a grant to attend school. Jose earned a degree in computer science within two years. During that time, he worked as a substitute teacher in Lawrence, and was dating Alina, his future wife, a fellow Cuban, who was working as an assistant principal in the same school system.

Jose went to Andover and began searching for a job. He spotted a beautiful, large glass building, so he took his resume and credentials and sought work. He didn't even know what the company did, but he loved the building. He handed his resume to the receptionist and said, "I want to work in this place."

"What position are you applying for?" the receptionist asked.

"I don't care. I'll do anything. I'll mop the floors or whatever you need. I just want to work in this beautiful building."

Less than a week later, Jose received a phone call from a man in the company's human resources department, asking him to come in for an interview.

Jose did. During the interview, the H.R. representative seemed interested in Jose and his credentials. "Is it correct that you speak English, Spanish, and Russian?" he asked. Jose affirmed that he could speak and write all three languages. At the close of the interview, the H.R. rep said, "With your qualifications, I think we can do something. I'll have my secretary give you a call."

A few days later, Jose received a call from that company offering him a job with a starting salary of $50,000 plus a $3,000 signing bonus! He became a video conferencing support engineer, working with some of the largest corporations in America and around the world. His boss encouraged him to further his education at the company's expense. Within six months, Jose earned certification as one of the top engineers in the company. He continued to advance up the corporate ladder, when one day the man who hired Jose—who was now a vice president of the company—invited him into his office.

"Have you ever wondered why and how you got hired here?"

"No, sir."

The company official pulled out the letter of recommendation written by the Guantanamo Bay Navy hospital commander.

"For twenty-five years in the Navy, I worked for the man who gave you this letter, and my last mission as a Navy captain was to help pick up refugees fleeing from Cuba," the VP said. "When I saw your resume, I didn't care if you knew anything about our business or not. I knew your capabilities and I wanted somebody like you working for us."

Jose went on to become an IT specialist for the governor of Tennessee, and later a commercial construction contractor and a builder of hotel properties. Within ten years, he was a millionaire. After leaving Cuba penniless with nothing but the clothes on his back, Jose Orozco is now an affluent businessman, working with Addiction Centers of America, helping us to design and develop our new high-end treatment facilities.

Although Jose has never been addicted to anything other than a positive attitude and hard work, he is a perfect example of believable hope. When anyone tells Jose that life is tough, or that his or her circumstances are hopeless, that it is impossible to get ahead, he responds, "Poverty and misery is a mental attitude; it is a state of mind. You can improve your life. If every day your goal is to do better than you did the day before, tomorrow is going to be a better day, and you are headed for glory. Establish the habit of looking for 'Yes.' Rather than thinking negatively, I believe that people and situations will turn out to be positive. Never blame anyone else for your condition, but instead, work hard and try to earn respect, and help everybody you can help."

Jose reminds people that what they need to do is find believable hope, visualize the life you want, surround yourself with winners, put your plans into action, and don't let setbacks or anything else hold you back and steal your dream.

Find Your Own Inner Peace

Whether through faith and prayer or some other means, it is important that you have something stronger than yourself upon which you can rely for inner strength to maintain your recovery. That's why you will often hear individuals who attend support groups such as AA or DRA talking about a Higher Power. Keep in mind that it is *your* own inner peace that you seek, not that which is foisted upon you by someone else. You must find what works best for you.

While on vacation, I went to see a movie, *Kung Fu Panda 2*, with our children and our friend's children. I was expecting the usual child-like schmaltz, but was pleasantly surprised to discover that the movie was really about the lead character finding inner peace before trying to defeat any external enemies. Po the panda and his friends were in a battle to save China from a vicious peacock who wanted to eliminate Kung Fu, but Po first had to come to terms with his past. He didn't realize that his family members had been taken away and killed by the bad guy. He sought help from his stepfather, a crane, and his dad helped him to deal with the death of his family members. It was only after Po the panda found inner peace himself that he was able to overcome and defeat the opposition forces in his life.

The message of the movie resonated with me, and it is good advice as we seek to transform our lives by changing our mindsets and developing believable hope. Being happy with where you are; doing good deeds and living with integrity; not lying, cheating, or stealing—living right—and being content with who you are . . . all are part of believable hope. Finding inner peace does not mean that you condone the misconduct of others. But you must focus on your own healing. Only then can you maintain the life you love, or help someone else get well.

Celebrate Your Maintenance

Unrealistic expectations can be a drawback, so remember: No one is perfect, not you, or the person you hope to help, and certainly not me. We are all somewhere in process, as we journey through life. An important key to maintaining the life you love is responding correctly to setbacks. When you slip up, remind yourself of your game plan and take whatever steps are necessary to reestablish positive patterns in your life. The use of incentives, positive affirmations, and small rewards for preestablished periods of success can be helpful as well.

For instance, Alcoholics Anonymous presents coins that are "won" by months and years of being sober, and other awards for achieving each year of sobriety. Establish some rewards for "good behavior," some targets to shoot at, plan a prize or special treat for each incremental goal you attain. These celebrations don't have to be expensive or exotic; it is the recognition that comes from achieving the goal that is important.

Joe Gibbs, one of the National Football League's most legendary coaches, won three Super Bowl trophies with the Washington Redskins. Joe often motivated multimillion-dollar players, including big, burly linemen or highly paid running backs, with relatively inexpensive rewards. To the best player of the week, Joe sometimes awarded a Sony Walkman, which at the time was state of the art—or the opportunity to drive his truck for a week. It wasn't the size or monetary value of the reward. It was the recognition the players received for winning the reward that cranked their motors. In the same way, by recognizing your progress and achievements you can keep yourself motivated and better maintain your new lifestyle.

Beware Cockiness or Complacency

Once you are free and clean, you can't get cocky or complacent, thinking temptation will never affect you again. It is always there, lurking in the shadows. But how you respond to setbacks will make all the difference.

Truly happy people are those who feel they are in control of their lives; they are not living at the whim of somebody or something else. Focus on what you want, where you want to go, but stay alert for potential pitfalls. It is not an either-or situation; it is a both-and situation. You need to keep moving forward, but always be wary of the areas where you might be vulnerable. Keep pressing forward in the new life you want, but keep your eyes open for slippery slopes that could send you reeling if you are not careful.

And remember, failures are merely stepping-stones to success. As Naomi Judd says, "A dead end is simply a good place to turn around."

My confident hope for you is that you will:

Develop believable hope.

Visualize the new world you want to create.

Surround yourself with winners.

Put your plan into action.

Maintain the life you love, as you anticipate and plan for relapses.

These same five principles comprise my personal belief system, and I've seen it work "miracles" in the lives of others. I've used these ideas to get off drugs and alcohol, to help overcome mental illness, and they work with weight loss, or other compulsive or life-controlling issues as well.

I encourage you to build your life on believable hope; you will be forever changed. Real lasting change is possible. The big question is: Are you ready and willing to get started?

> Man often becomes what he believes himself to be. If I say to myself that I cannot do a certain thing, it is possible that I may end by becoming incapable of doing it. On the contrary, if I have the belief that I can do it, I shall surely acquire the capacity to do it, even if I may not have it at the beginning.
>
> —*Mahatma Gandhi*

Plant Good Seed

Anyone who has ever planted a garden or attempted to grow some flowers in the yard knows that good results take time and care. You must plant your seed and then give it the necessary nutrients, water, light, and time to grow. Changing your mindset requires a renewed self-concept, and that will not happen overnight. It will take time and regular applications of accurate information, inspiration, and encouragement. But it can happen, as you consistently make wise choices and maintain your new mindset. As Grandma Cartwright often told me, "You really do reap what you sow."

Keep nurturing the person you want to be. No longer regarding yourself as an addict, alcoholic, a compulsive overeater, or any other negative-emotion-evoking term, you can dare to see yourself clean, sober, free, and at a healthy weight; with good, constructive friends; and enjoying a positive lifestyle.

You have a lot of good things going for you. Don't allow anyone or anything to deter you from achieving your goals. Letting go of the past and looking forward to good things, expect to win, do the hard work to succeed, to live a healthy and whole life—and your life will be filled with believable hope!

QUESTIONS About
MAINTAINING THE LIFE YOU LOVE

1. List a few situations you are likely to encounter where substances to which you are vulnerable might be in use (e.g., parties, former hangouts). How will you choose to avoid those compromising situations or triggers that could lead you to unhealthy choices?

_____

_____

_____

_____

_____

_____

2. Since relapse is normal, our goal is love and tolerance of others and most importantly, of ourselves. Make this your new standard: *Progress, not Perfection.* List several ways you hope to make progress and enjoy life within the next twelve months.

1. _____

2. _____

3. _____

4. _____

3. In what areas do you need to practice the most (*physical, mental/ emotional, intellectual, relationships, financial, spiritual*)? What practices might help you improve in these areas?

_____

_____

_____

_____

4. List several strategies you have learned from this book that have been most helpful to you.

_____

_____

_____

_____

5. A key element of recovery is to get your focus off yourself and help someone else. List three people you know who need some believable hope, and consider what you might be able to do to help each person.

1. _____

_____

_____

2. _____

_____

_____

3. _____

_____

_____

WE'RE HERE
TO HELP

Do you have a drug or alcohol problem? Are you suffering from prolonged depression? Are you trying to lose weight or maintain your weight loss? We can provide you with all the tools necessary, including a game plan that works and the daily encouragement you need to stick with your plan. Come spend a day with us, or a week, or a month, or as long as it takes—we will not give up on you; and we will encourage you to overcome every obstacle standing in the way of your becoming the person you want to be.

If you or a loved one needs help, you can explore the various programs we have to offer by visiting our website at BelievableHope.com or calling toll free, 866/391/4244.

NOTES

[1] Interview with Skip Prichard, "Are You Low on Rocket Fuel?" Skip Prichard Leadership Insights, April 19, 2012. © Skip Prichard, 2012, 1 Ingram Blvd., LaVergne, TN 37086.

[2] *Piers Morgan Tonight*, "An Interview with Anthony Hopkins; Discussion of Exorcism," February 5, 2011, http://transcripts.cnn.com/TRANSCRIPTS/1102/05/pmt.0.

[3] Dan Cronin, interview with author, April 27, 2012.

[4] Wayne W. Dyer, *Wishes Fulfilled* (Carlsbad, CA: Hay House, 2012), 26.

[5] Neville Goddard, *The Power of Awareness* (Camarillo, CA: DeVorss Publications, 2005), 12.

[6] Dyer, *Wishes Fulfilled*, 32–33.

[7] Goddard, *Power of Awareness*, 63–64.

[8] Adapted from Dyer, *Wishes Fulfilled*, 74–76.

[9] Sandra Simpson LeSourd, *The Compulsive Woman* (Old Tappan, NJ: Chosen Books, 1987), 41.

[10] Rick Warren, Twitter, October 6, 2011.

[11] Kitty Dukakis with Jane Scovell, *Now You Know* (New York: Simon & Schuster, 1990), 9.

[12] Buzz Aldrin with Ken Abraham, *Magnificent Desolation* (New York: Harmony Books, Random House, 2009), 173.

[13] See Mark 9:17–23 (NKJV).

About
Michael Cartwright

Michael Cartwright is a respected addiction industry trailblazer and a noted behavioral healthcare entrepreneur. Over his seventeen-year career, Michael has been instrumental in setting up addiction treatment centers across the United States, which have served over 20,000 patients. He has been committed to research-based treatment and has directly supervised fifteen federally funded studies that helped lay the foundation for the 5 Elements to overcome any addiction. A leading advocate for dual diagnosis treatment, Michael was nominated by Senator Ted Kennedy to the Senate Health Committee. He was a founding board member for the 12-Step organization Dual Recovery Anonymous, a national support group helping people suffering from combined mental health and substance abuse issues. He currently serves as the Chairman of the Board of American Addiction Centers, a behavioral healthcare company with treatment centers in California, Texas, Nevada, and Tennessee. For more information, contact www.BelievableHope.com.

INDEX